CONVERSATIONS IN GLOBAL ANGLICAN THEOLOGY
Faith

Edited by
MICHAEL BATTLE

With Contributions by
THANDI GAMEDZE
ROSE HUDSON-WILKIN
HENRY MBAYA
THOKOZILE J. MBAYA
THABO MAKGOBA
SIMON CHUL LAI RO
STEPHEN SPENCER
WILHELM VERWOERD

Foreword by
ROWAN WILLIAMS

Seabury Books
NEW YORK

Seabury Books
19 East 34th Street
New York, NY 10016
www.churchpublishing.org

Seabury Books is an imprint of Church Publishing Incorporated

Cover design by Tessa Wright Design
Typeset by Nord Compo

ISBN 978-1-64065-742-7 (paperback)
ISBN 978-1-64065-743-4 (hardback)
ISBN 978-1-64065-744-1 (eBook)

Library of Congress Control Number: 2024944117

Contents

Contributors

The Rev. Michael Battle, Ph.D.
President of the Peace Battle Institute, USA
Extraordinary Professor at the Desmond Tutu Centre for Religion
and Social Justice, the University of the Western Cape, South
Africa of the University of the Western Cape, South Africa
And Theologian in Community at Trinity Church in the City of Boston

Dr. Thandi Gamedze
A leader at the The Warehouse and BottomUp.
Post-doc fellowship at the University of the Western Cape's Desmond
Tutu Centre for Religion and Social Justice
Lecturer at University of Cape Town's School of Education
South Africa

Bishop Rose Hudson-Wilkin
Bishop of Dover
Diocese of Canterbury
United Kingdom

Archbishop Dr. Thabo Makgoba
Anglican Church of Southern Africa
Ph.D. University of Cape Town
South Africa

Professor Henry Mbaya
Theology Faculty
Stellenbosch University
South Africa

Thokozile J. Mbaya, Ph.D. Student
VID Specialized University, Stavanger, Norway

Dean Simon Ro Chul Lai
Dean of Graduate School of Theology
Graduate School of Theology
Sungkonghoe (Anglican) University
South Korea

The Revd. Canon Dr. Stephen Spencer
Adviser on Theological Education and Lambeth Conference
    Implementation
Canon of Musoma Cathedral, Mara, Tanzania
United Kingdom

Wilhelm Verwoerd
(grandson of Hendrik Verwoerd, South African Prime Minister and
    the architect of apartheid)
Senior Research Associate & Facilitator | AVReQ (Centre for the
    Study of the Afterlife of Violence and the Reparative Quest)
Stellenbosch University
South Africa

Foreword

Part of the destructive legacy of a Western-dominated pattern of mission activity is a deficit of trust. The history of Christian activity in general and Anglican history in particular is shadowed by the memory of evangelists saying, "Trust us" to non-European communities—and then colluding with (or sometimes actively promoting) the deepest betrayals of trust. And that memory is going to color so much of what is possible and impossible in sharing the Good News today. Whether it is the Atlantic slave trade, resistance to all sorts of aspects of indigenous liberation in various contexts, the draconian repression of cultural identities in residential schools, or whatever else, there is no denying that the body count is, literally, high as a result of the whole huge and complex project of European migration and domination, with Christian rhetoric regularly conscripted into the process.

But—to anticipate the outraged protests of people who think that saying this out loud is some kind of betrayal of the gospel itself—this does not mean either that the gospel is completely paralyzed and powerless in the hands of its Western advocates, or that the colonial project was the only source of evil and injustice in an otherwise sunny and peaceful world. Another part of the legacy of mission is the recognition that countless non-European communities found in Christian faith a vision of the world that equipped them to challenge not only the problematic aspects of their own heritage but the evils of colonial power itself. It's often been said that one of the most important gifts of the Christian Church is the capacity to train its own critics (usually without quite noticing that this is what it's doing). We can continue to celebrate the gospel as a word of release, absolution and empowerment—"the *authority* to become children of God," as the opening chapter of John's Gospel firmly declares—while also recognizing gratefully how that word sets us free to see our own history truthfully and with penitence. The gospel commends itself by showing just how insistently it pushes its way through the overgrown thickets of cultural and political manipulation to open up new horizons.

But to go back for a moment to the issue of trust: central to the proclamation of the Good News of God in Jesus Christ is the statement that God is to be trusted. God's raising from the dead of the rejected and murdered prophet of the Kingdom shows that God's purpose of creating a boundaryless community of mutual service, delight, compassion and companionship is not altered by human betrayals of any kind. The risen Jesus is, as St. Paul memorably says, the "Yes!" to all God's promises, to Jew and Gentile, neighbor and stranger. Our worship, our study of Scripture, our celebration of the Lord's Supper, all these are ultimately ways for God to tell us once again that God is to be trusted, that God's commitment to the world is unchangeable and invincible. *Faith* is essentially just this vision; the formulations of creed and liturgy are all rooted in the struggle to find ways of talking to God and about God that do some sort of justice to this divine faithfulness. The acknowledgment of the divinity of Christ is the acknowledgment that what God does in Jesus, God always and unalterably does; and our historic faith in God as trinity flows from this.

And so the Church, if it seeks to share the gift it has been given, has to keep on asking not just, "Are we being faithful to what has been shown to us?" but also, "Are we showing ourselves to be faithful people—in the sense of people who can be trusted, who are committed to the world that God is committed to?" If we ask what the heart of discipleship is, we should answer that it is the struggle to show the face of a trustworthy God through the struggle to be trustworthy people. Recognizing just how far we as Church have fallen short of this, just how deeply we have betrayed, is a fundamental task for all of us, but very specially for those—like me—who have been formed by a long history of unexamined cultural power. We are not called to defend our record where it is indefensible, but to express our faith in divine faithfulness by facing truthfully our readiness to stifle, soften, distort or forget the heart of the gospel, and opening ourselves to the gift of those who have been made to suffer.

That is why a book like this is itself an act of faith. Those who have experienced the structures of the global Church—Anglican or any other kind—as a source of denial and silencing are saying with unmistakeable clarity that these structures cannot have the last word. They have faith in a Christian future, they show faithfulness to the realities of the social and cultural contexts from which they come, they even show faith that those with a more privileged history might be able to listen to them. They explore what it is they trust, and they invite others to trust them. The Anglican legacy is a tangled affair in so many ways, so deeply implicated in the projects of conquest, dominance and exploitation. Yet the Anglican family, with all its confusion, its shrill and polarized contemporary quarrels, its perennial temptation to think itself more significant than it is in all sorts of contexts, still manages to somehow nourish voices of insight, critical honesty and transformative spiritual depth. The series of which this book is the first grows out of this mysterious capacity, in a bruised and divided human community, with a seriously compromised history, to let itself be brought back to the heart of God's gift. May God grant that it will—to quote St. Paul once again, in the first chapter of Romans—speak "from faith to faith," speaking out of trust in God's fidelity to a world of suspicion and distance that is summoned to share and to create trust.

Rowan Williams
104th Archbishop of Canterbury
Cardiff
2024

Preface

This is the first volume of a new series exploring various facets of Anglican theology. The Anglican Communion, the third largest Christian communion with more than 85 million members, is said to rest authority on a "three-legged stool" of scripture, tradition, and reason, a notion traceable to the 16th century English theologian Richard Hooker. Other definitions of Anglicanism emphasize common prayer as its defining feature, while the Chicago-Lambeth Quadrilateral locates Anglicanism in the balance of Scripture, Creed, Sacrament, and the Episcopate. Other permutations of Anglicanism include Anglo-Catholic, evangelical, liberal, and conservative.

There is one constant throughout, however—namely, most of these descriptions of Anglicanism have historically assumed conformity to a White, Western world identity. And unfortunately, others who seek to live the Anglican faith in their contexts are often discounted as erroneous or inferior due to being in the Global South or to being a member of the wrong sexual orientation or gender. Because of these conflicting notions of what it means to be Anglican, the premise of this new series is that the global aspect of the Anglican Communion is better balanced on a four-legged stool. So, instead of the typical trilogy of scripture, tradition, and reason, this series presents a tetralogy of **Faith, Culture, Activism, and Mysticism** written by theologians and spiritual leaders around the world.

This four-volume series amplifies theological voices often kept silent by the western world's dominance over what is considered legitimate Anglican theology. These are powerful theologians, journalists, scholars, and spiritual writers, especially in the global south, who are often neglected by western publishing. They are not all Anglican, which is a blessing in disguise that will allow for viewpoints that move beyond echo chambers and affinity groups. In short, this series encourages theological reflection, especially from lesser-known areas of the Anglican Communion.

This series will demonstrate the need to pause, listen, and allow historically marginalized voices to speak to the authority of what (or who) holds us all together. Instead of waiting for crises to mobilize human societies, this series offers a preventative approach in imagining who we can become together. Each author in this tetralogy series will address some of these challenges— and hopefully facilitate some consensus around Communion and what it could eventually mean today.

My goal as the editor is to guard against theological tropes and stereotypes that often spawn from leisure societies in the Western world. My essential questions and convictions are:

- In light of colonial affliction around the world, what is the international community's role in fostering a global village?
- Considering the current civil wars in the Anglican Communion regarding who is legitimately a human being, we seem less equipped to offer light to this afflicted world.
- And given that the rules for globalization are usually set by the Western world (i.e. the economically wealthy), how do we localize the Anglican Communion with the day-to-day

concerns of parish life, partisan politics, the proliferation of drugs such as fentanyl, and a seemingly post-Covid world?

- Lastly, how do we practice Communion not only for "Anglicans" but for all of God's children?

My hope for this tetralogy series is that these kinds of questions, asked by deep thinkers around the world, will invite us all to a different kind of reign on earth that God offers to all of us, not just some. It is a reign in which we redefine who we are related to through non-zero-sum worldviews. Our series' authors address fundamental questions for what it means to be in Communion. They offer Anglicans and other human beings constructive theology for our exponential and ever changing contexts. Communion makes us all address the difficult question: How do we imagine a world in which no one needs to leave a homeland to survive? The world is looking for such guidance. It is my hope that this series provides specific and implementable answers that can deal with the many daily crises of our siblings around the world without waiting for new crises to occur.

I wish to thank Justin Hoffman for initiating the idea to produce a Seabury Book series on Anglican conversations. Our long discussion in my office at General Theological Seminary was inspiring to the point I resisted being Jonah in running away from this important work. Airié Stuart, Publisher at Church Publishing Incorporated, facilitated this final outcome for which I am indebted to her for her support and skill in making this first book in the series a success. Mark Powers provided timely production of this work; and with great patience ensured that valuable voices made it into this text. I also need to acknowledge Tyler Simnick for his acumen to expose this book as widely as possible. It must also be stated here that this book would not have been completed without the corralling efforts of Katherine Lim. Thank you, Katherine! Of course, it goes without saying that the contributors to this book are the reason that we are reading this preface. They are not only fantastic leaders in the world but also incredible people that you, the audience of this book, would do well to have lead conferences and programs where you are.

Introduction

Originally, this first volume on Faith in the series of Anglican Conversations was entitled, *Ex Nihilo: Fostering Theological Voices Post Apartheid.* However, due to the intersectional nature of global concern around patterns of apartheid and xenophobia, the book expanded its boundaries and geographical borders. The concern of this book, however, remains the same as it attempts to answer the question: How can **we** enable authentic conversations around the practice of faith in a global context in which many theologians and spiritual leaders in the Global South are often relegated toward a ministry focus only context or a social activism context. This binary is fueled by the western occupation of commercialized books and journals compartmentalized by discrete discourse. In this western world approach, the arduous task of being approved as legitimate writers and thinkers is based solely upon western gatekeepers of what is a legitimate text as well as legitimate thought. So, again, how can we enable authentic conversations in the Anglican communion? The "we" implied in this question are Anglican clergy and laity, concerned about the lack of public theological discourse represented by a diverse array of theological discourse coming from around the Anglican Communion and not just the UK and North America. Among the "we" is also the need of producing more theologians for the church, a difficult task given the new opportunities of post-colonial societies in the global south in which one need no longer aspire to be a priest or teacher as one's highest educational goal.

It is said that one of the victims of apartheid is the role of theologian, who was perceived as more ornamental in the crucial fight against it. What were more vital were activist priests and laity, not reflective priests and laity. In the 1980s, however, there were organizations that tried to practice the harmony of action and reflection such as the Institute for Contextual Theology that provided reflection and produced the Kairos document. Currently, in post-Apartheid South Africa, it is rare to find the above harmony between action and reflection. For example, it is rare to find clergy with published writing or theologians active in the church. A rift increases between those who practice theology in the written form and those who practice theology through the Mother's Union.

"To find time to write is a luxury," is the reason once given to me by several South African clergy. Such a cultural perception of the theologian has created a dearth of intellectual material among global Anglicans and global Christians (hopefully, these two identities are not mutually exclusive). Anglican leaders around the Communion, ironically, are similar to South African students. Both have learned to negotiate their identities and roles in relation to activism against apartheid. Now that apartheid has formally toppled in South Africa, at least legally, theological reflection is difficult for theological students and the same for spiritual leaders to reflect and write if there is no similar monolith to reflect against. Courtney Sampson, the previous chaplain to the University of the Western Cape and subsequent Electoral Commission of South Africa's provincial electoral officer for the Western Cape, once told me about the struggle of current university students in South Africa to be real students as opposed to political agitators. "It's boring to just study books and stay in school through the full duration."[1] Those who have learned to understand self in relation to struggle do not know who they are if the struggle ceases, it no longer exists or cannot change course. This existential situation remains with global Christians who are used to ministry, action, and protest and often find it artificial and irrelevant to write and reflect on matters of faith. Perhaps, this lack of reflection among global Christians is due to the normal scenario of activist and those grounded in various kinds of practical struggle to be human. In which case, global and Anglican conversations on topics like faith, culture, activism, and mysticism will speak not only to the South African context but also to much of Christendom where the dichotomy exists between "learned clergy and laity" and "socially active clergy and laity."

The aim of this first book on faith, therefore, is to counter the notion that reflection and writing are somehow luxurious. We present these reflections, if for no other reason, than that the catholic church needs to know about the significant role that Anglicans and Christians have played in applying Christian faith in a context of intolerable, racial oppression. The methodology of this book is to exemplify global voices in order to recover the balance between action and reflection. This methodology is justified through the historical examples of Anglican clergy in South Africa who demonstrated the need to hold action

---

1. Discussed with the Rev. Courtney Sampson in 1993 during my stay with Archbishop Desmond Tutu. Courtney is now rightfully acknowledged as and awarded the 2023 Hubert Walter Award for Reconciliation and Interfaith Co-operation by the Archbishop of Canterbury.

and reflection in tension. One may think of Albert Luthuli, Trevor Huddleston, and Desmond Tutu. Because of such a list, Anglicans have developed an international reputation for significant Christian theology able to address and affect social practices. The particularity of Anglican clergy and laity is important for the global context in that their historical witness produces an international audience, all of whom discover the disjuncture between church and society in how each acts and reflects. One of the great insights of this book given to the reader is how the synthesis of action and reflection emerges in which to do is to pray. The particularity is the Anglican church, but this particularity serves in an iconic and sacramental capacity to help Christians in various contexts develop consensus on how to discern to be the church today and tomorrow.

The authors of the essays in this book are significant Anglican clergy and laity as well as spiritual leaders beyond Anglicanism who recognize this synthesis that to do is to pray. They are astute, however, in recognizing the dilemma of action and reflection set forth so far in this introduction. They address this dilemma through their various and diverse passions and yet they find consensus in the fact that practices of faith must be maintained to reflect on what has been done so as to act more mercifully, clearly, and justly. We imagine you the audience to be the same. Envisioned for this book are socially conscious spiritual leaders all over the world who are also struggling with the dilemma of action and reflection. Many such leaders especially recognize their own failings to reflect on their "right" actions.

Authors have been chosen on the basis of their authority and passion on the subject pertaining to Christian faith as practiced in South Africa, South Korea, and the UK. Also, each author has demonstrated faith in their particular contexts by providing a synthesis between reflection and action. We begin in Part One on Anglican Identity and Faith with Bishop Rose Hudson-Wilkin, Bishop of Dover in England, who reflects upon pastoral experience in the growing schism and scapegoating of communities and individuals who often misunderstand the faith commitments of today and only fixate on one day out of the week. Bishop Rose, a Black female bishop of Jamaican origin, has an unusual aerial view of the Anglican church as she serves the Church of England in the unique capacity as Bishop of Dover and in a de facto capacity the geography of Canterbury, the destination of Anglican pilgrims. She is the first Black woman to become a Church of England bishop. She was previously Chaplain to the Speaker of the House of Commons from 2010 to 2019, having trained with the Church Army before entering parish ministry.

When she refers to knowing a large majority of people, such a metric is not merely anecdotal but actual as well. In her chapter, she provides a sermonic memoir of her experience with large swaths of people seeking faith. She cautions, though, that such faith should not stop within the literal walls of a church building. For many Christians, she writes, "Their duty is done until they return to their place of worship a day or a week later. For many like them, faith is simply all about the activity of worship. So, the question to ask is, "what happens in the interim?' From the moment they leave that designated place of worship, what next?"

Bishop Rose's thoughtful reflection enhances this first book of Anglican conversations in that she challenges the unhealthy assumptions that faith somehow is pavlovian in its confined association to a time on Sunday morning or a building of gothic architecture. For her, it is not good enough to say we have faith, especially a faith which is inward-looking. Faith must be alive and identified by our actions. A good way to know such faith is through the interrogation of our baptisms in which three prominent questions are asked: Do you turn to Christ? Do you repent of your sins? Do you renounce evil? The baptized, the congregation, and even the godparents who may not be avowed Christians respond in the affirmative to turning to Christ, repenting of sins, and renouncing evil.

As a bishop with an aerial view of congregations, Bishop Rose is careful to point out that these statements are not just to be said once at a baptismal service and then forgotten. They must be answered daily! She also reminds her gathered congregations or her flock that the infant child will not understand the meaning of the symbolisms being used at the baptismal service; neither will they know what love, forgiveness, and compassion look like unless they see it in action. Bishop Rose's insight here is that Christians are introduced to faith through baptism. The baptismal fonts in most churches are to be found near to the entrance of the church, thus symbolising baptism being the start of one's introduction of the Christian faith.

In her ministry as an Anglican bishop, she spends time visiting deaneries which are geographical areas with several churches within their borders. During these visits, she conducts what she affectionately calls "In Conversation with Bishop Rose." Invariably, she recalls in her chapter here, one of the questions repeatedly asked is, "What is the greatest challenge to the church at this present time?" Based upon Bishop Rose's insight, she responds, "A lack of confident Christians." Herein is the power of her chapter—namely, by confident Christians, she refers to those who know that they believe in a living God who loves all of humanity and creation. This God lives within those who are hungry and thirsty, sick and in prison, and naked, needing something as basic as to be clothed. It takes faith to know and see such a God. Bishop Rose helps us to see that faith is more than the labels we carry judging each other. She concludes in her chapter that faith is:

> . . . . deep touching deep! If faith is going to matter, it must go beyond: "I am anglo-catholic, I am evangelical, I am liberal catholic, I am an open evangelical, I am liberal, I am a conservative evangelical, and the list goes on. . ." We seem to invest more in these labels than in the Good News. We gather like-minded people around us and we form cliques locking others out. In the midst of this all, we forget why we worship and indeed who we worship. We become blinded by our own desires not the desires of our Lord and Saviour. We also become self-serving, propping up our newly built castles.

Continuing in Part One on Anglican Identity and faith, our next author also lives in the context of the Church of England but has traveled around the Anglican Communion. He is the Rev. Canon Dr Stephen Spencer, Adviser on Theological Education in the Anglican Communion and Lambeth Conference Implementation, and Canon of Musoma

Cathedral, Mara, Tanzania. Spencer reflects upon the essence of the Anglican Communion both in a crisis situation as well as in the burgeoning situations in which diverse persons and communities move toward closer proximity. Local diversities and the formation of national churches experienced the growth of provinces, archdioceses, and metropolitan jurisdictions. Despite perennial tensions caused by growth, over time Anglican churches largely continue to participate in the life of the global communion. The mantra of hope seems to be a cry to embrace the need for interdependence without relinquishing autonomy. Spencer cautions, however, that local autonomy, which has become the hallmark of Anglican ecclesiology, has sometimes led to real difficulties.

In Spencer's chapter, he provides insights into how mechanisms for a central intervention have sometimes been impossible to resolve matters of conflict in the Anglican Communion. For example, disagreements over the place of the Biblical; disagreements over how to respond to polygamists, then disagreements over the ordination of women, and most recently, disagreements over whether to bless same-sex unions have all increased the recognized role for four instruments of communion. In the Anglican Communion, such instruments are: the Archbishop of Canterbury, the Lambeth Conference, the Anglican Consultative Council, and the Primates' Meeting. These bodies, Spencer believes, could be likened to musical instruments, each having its own distinctive voice, but their role is to work with each other to contribute to the harmony of the whole.

More recently, Anglicans have interpreted the work of the Anglican Communion in terms of the Five Marks of Mission for which the instruments of Communion are intended to serve. As the Anglican Communion website states, these Marks of Mission are:

1. To proclaim the Good News of the Kingdom
2. To teach, baptize and nurture new believers
3. To respond to human need by loving service
4. To transform unjust structures of society, to challenge violence of every kind and pursue peace and reconciliation
5. To strive to safeguard the integrity of creation, and sustain and renew the life of the earth

Spencer provides the reader first-hand knowledge and the experience of wrestling with the notion and context of the Anglican Communion. Despite the many challenges such Communion facts, there is the good news around the Communion that women's ordination is increasingly gaining ground in every continent and many Anglo-Catholics and Evangelicals who initially opposed it are now supportive of it.

The search for consensus has not succeeded in so far as who is quintessentially an Anglican, but some progress in terms of the diversity of the image of God among humanity is indeed taking place. Spencer provides an important short-hand history of the Anglican Communion in his chapter and provides just as importantly authoritative references at the end of his chapter. What is important here is in how an official leader in the Anglican Communion office points to how God's mission is no longer being seen as descriptions of different church activities but as descriptions of the way God's people participate in the coming of Christ's reign on earth. Spencer rightly concludes that future decades will reveal if this paradigm continues to grow and become embedded or whether alternative hierarchical paradigms reassert themselves in different regions of the world.

Lastly, in Part One on Anglican identity and faith, and reflecting on the Anglican Communion for how static contexts can move into dynamic existence, Dean Simon Ro Chul Lai, Dean of the Graduate School of Theology at Sungkonghoe (Anglican) University in Seoul, Korea, reflects upon the changing vocation of Anglican identity as it explores the integrity of new calls as well as the insight of where some Anglican churches and individuals may be wandering in the wilderness. Ro believes that the concept of Christian covenant rests on the relationship between God and God's people, the Church. In other words, when all is said and done the church must witness to a steadfast love for the world. The reason for this, according to Ro, is that any Anglican ecclesiology or study of the church must describe a dynamic Anglican understanding of the nature of covenant as expressing the life of the triune God's dynamic relationships.

This suggests that the Anglican Communion is not static and should not dissolve into a legal transaction and agreement for its own sake. The Anglican Communion should regard covenant as a way of being the Church, participating in the very life of the triune God's dynamic relationships. As Ro offers reflection on the life of the Anglican Communion during the Windsor Covenant's emphasis on a structural approach to the maintenance of the Communion, our Anglican conversations should always reflect the life of the triune God's dynamic relationships.

Ro also offers the helpful insight that the Anglican Communion should always take into account the contemplative dimension of the nature of God in order to see how we reciprocate the image of God. Most importantly, whatever the presenting issues may be, the imposition of a static structural approach on the ongoing life of the Anglican Communion is incompatible with both an Anglican understanding of the nature of covenant and authority. It is also not helpful in resolving the future crises in the Communion. This raises the question of where static kinds of Anglican structures of Communion come from. Ro concludes that static thinking about the Communion, implies the concept of Anglican tribal identity, which lies behind any kind of non-dynamic and non-relational thinking about Anglican identity.

When Anglican identity is understood as a communion, then we reflect the life of the triune God's dynamic relationships which far surpass exponential change in that there is more of an assumption that God miraculously creates ex nihilo. Therefore, no static criteria for who is the church or what is the Anglican identity should be forced on the Anglican Communion. Here, Ro concludes accordingly that the centrality of the life of Anglican identity as Communion allows the Anglican Communion to hold to its inclusive attitude towards differences within the Communion. We need to work to remain open to God's final purpose of embracing all creation in the world. We need to remain open to a new way of thinking about Anglican identity as Communion that creates a hospitable and open space for all.

Ro's contribution here is to be the voice crying in the wilderness to guard against fragmentation and polarization in situations of conflict by separating the ordering of Communion from the triune God's dynamic relationships which are the source and ground of the life of the Anglican Communion at all levels. It is too easy to settle upon the expediency of a static theological climate in the institutional church, thereby predefining and polarising issues like same-sex unions, immigration, and laisse-faire economics. We easily create barriers between parties and individuals in the Anglican Communion if we lack the plasticity in understanding the dynamic circumstances of living in exponential change.

In Part 2 on the Particularity of Anglican identity and Faith in South Africa, our next author is indeed a representative of what the current and future paradigm of theology will look like. She is Dr. Thandi Gamedze, who reflects upon the impact of organizing women in the church. When she speaks, she represents thousands of South African women's voices that often are obfuscated by male-dominant voices. Her chapter draws upon research to provide a description and analysis of the ways that White dominance persists and is reinscribed today. In so doing, she explores the dilemma that this poses for Black people and their faith within the church. Finally, drawing on both the testimonies of Black people within these church realities, as well as histories of those who have navigated similar faith dynamics, she explores the ways in which Black people navigate White institutional Christianity to carve out paths for liberating and liberated faith.

Gamedze is quick to point out that in writing her chapter, which uses race as a central analytical concept, she want to ensure that she is not reproducing racialized forms of consciousness through an uncritical acceptance of apartheid racial categories. As scholars of critical race theory teach, she believes, race is a social construction created and employed for the purposes of oppression and exploitation. This is vitally important because of the systems built around this social construct, particularly that of racial capitalism upon which colonialism and apartheid in South Africa were built. Race continues to carry political, social, and economic relevance in society and in the church's struggle of faith.

Gamedze provides invaluable insight for how Christianity and its expressions across contexts have alienated and subjugated Black people. She also provides insight into the various mechanisms through which a colonial imagination of Christian faith has been resisted and Black faith reclaimed. In the South African context, as well as beyond, this history is full of these stories of faith reclamation. The tragedy here is in how these are histories that are often hidden and removed from those fighting similar battles to reclaim their faith today.

She concludes with a Christian imagination in which it would be wonderful if churches upholding White institutional space would repent of this, renounce it, and take radical material steps towards creating something different. And yet, she has the faith to know that failing this, Black faith, as it always has, will live on as Black Christians soldier on as their ancestors did in a myriad of ways. In short, Christians around the world affected by colonial worldviews must do the faithful work to build and fight for a faith that is both liberated and liberating for all who are oppressed.

Given this exponential change in history, the next author in Part 2, explores the Particularity of Anglican Identity and Faith in South Africa, and carefully takes the reader through the Anglican church in South Africa's fight for human equity. He is Professor Thokozile (Henry) J Mbaya who reflects on the delayed resolution of the full inclusion of gay and lesbian identity in the church. Mbaya digests for the reader important historical resources in understanding major Anglican leaders like Bishop John Colenso (1814-1883), who fought valiantly for the human dignity of Zulu culture and was excommunicated for such efforts, precipitating the first Lambeth Conference.

From this starting point, Mbaya takes the reader through the Anglican global debate on human sexuality at the Lambeth Conferences. On the topic of human sexuality, these Conferences called on each province to reassess its stance towards persons of homosexual orientation, considering human rights and the need for pastoral concern. These Conferences did not end the debate, especially for progressive provinces like the Anglican Church of Southern Africa. In 2008, human sexuality was debated in Jerusalem, resulting in the GAFCON Jerusalem Declaration, a doctrinal statement formulated by the Global Anglican Future Conference (GAFCON), an international group of conservative Anglican leaders and churches which affirms that marriage is between one man and one woman, intended by God to be a lifelong union.

Where Mbaya's chapter is important in our Anglican conversations, is in how on the African continent responses to gay clergy and same-sex relationships have been very negative. The dilemma of Ubuntu arises. Ubuntu is an African worldview that emphasizes being human through other people. The concept is understood by seeing individuals as being inextricably linked and connected to others—a concept that Archbishop Tutu made famous. Unfortunately, such a worldview when related to the human rights of gay and lesbian persons seems to fall short. Mbaya looks at the efforts of Archbishop Thabo Makgoba to bridge such a gap as well as the valiant witness of Mpho Tutu van Furth (Archbishop Tutu's youngest child) who married her same-sex partner, Marceline van Furth, in 2015. Mbaya concludes that Tutu-van Furth deserves equity. From the Ubuntu point of view, denial of their sexuality and marriage violates the spirit to be free and human.

Part 2 on the Particularity of Anglican Identity and Faith in South Africa also contains a powerful reflection from Wilhelm Verwoerd, the grandson of Hendrik Verwoerd, South African Prime Minister and the architect of apartheid. He contemplates what justice looks like given his family's background in complicity with apartheid. Currently, Verwoerd serves as Senior Researcher and facilitator, the Centre for the Study of the Afterlife of Violence and the Reparative Quest (AVReQ), Stellenbosch University, South Africa. He reflects upon the marginalized White South African identity and the dilemma of being a White minority in Africa. Verwoerd begins his chapter with his encounter with a unsettling painting in an Anglican cathedral, nearly forty years ago. He was working as a researcher in the Truth and Reconciliation Commission (TRC) office in Cape Town and regularly attended services in the nearby St George's

Anglican Cathedral. After a special reconciliation service, on 16 November 1997, his attention was drawn to a big painting in one corner of the cathedral. It was indeed unusual to see the Christ figure depicted as a Black person. Verwoerd recognized the face of Chief Albert Luthuli, former president of the ANC and Nobel Peace Prize winner. But his eyes were drawn to a figure in the bottom left corner: a White soldier with a long spear piercing the side of the Black figure on the cross. That White soldier was his grandfather, Hendrik Verwoerd. His grandfather was stabbing the Black Christ.

In his chapter, Verwoerd reflects on the trauma of seeing his grandfather in such a graphic way. The saving grace was in having a "pastoral tea" conversation with Archbishop Tutu. For the grandson Verwoerd, Tutu highlighted how the radical nature of Ubuntu midwifed Verwoerd's rebirth as a White Afrikaner. Verwoerd was transformed with an embodied commitment to follow Christ in post-1994 South Africa. He then continues the conversation with Tutu, by revisiting Tutu's warning to not take on a "burden that is unbearable" and instead draw upon the practice of communal repair.

In his chapter Verwoerd highlights how the transformation rather than the transmission of the "sins of the fathers" require the transformation of one's sense of self. At the political level, this re-formation includes going beyond an individualistic, liberal sense of self towards an expanded self that accepts generational inextricability. And transforming "from a spiritual depth" includes internalising an incarnational sense of self. This depth dimension enables one's embodiment to become bearable through a coming home to one's body as, foundationally, another "temple of the Holy Spirit" (1 Cor 6:19). Doing lectio divina with this awe-inspiring metaphor of body as temple takes him beyond moralistic reduction of a puritanical warning against body-based "sins," towards an apophatic sense of self, with indwelling divine beyondness providing the unbreakable, all-embracing heart of human beyondness.

In Verwoerd's conclusion, the deep transformation of the pain represented by his White embodiment also requires a complementary anchoring in the cross and *Black Christ*. Verwoerd grounds his contemplative practice in the mystery of the cross, aided by Cynthia Bourgeault. For her centering prayer is, theologically speaking, about following Jesus on his incarnational path of *kenosis* (Phil 2:9-16). This apophatic prayer practice is a daily practice. It is a participation in the death of Christ but also a participation in his resurrection. Centering prayer gradually becomes ingrained in us. In understanding what is specifically required of him as a White Verwoerd, the *Black Christ*, mediated by Tutu and others, has helped Verwoerd to follow Jesus in the "outer world" of post-1994 South Africa.

Anchoring Part 2 and the entirety of this book of Anglican conversations on faith, Archbishop Thabo Makgoba writes a chapter on African interdependence and the impact of such reflection on the future life of the African Church. These Anglican conversations are blessed to have Makgoba's vantage point at the southern tip of Africa, as he reflects upon the interstices of the world that continues to go through epoch-making changes such as in revolutionary technological advances which have the power to achieve great good but could also threaten to tear humanity apart. We are also witnessing an explosive growth of racist and xenophobic expressions of nationalism and authoritarian right-wing populist politics in many different regions of the world. There is also the growth of an unbridled capitalism.

For Makgoba, the major question is, what do we as Anglicans, as Christians, as people of faith, and as human beings have to offer our world as we navigate the 21st century? More specifically, he asks, what do those of us from the Global South have to offer the Anglican Communion and the ecumenical and inter-faith communities as we all struggle together to discern the mission and the ministry to which God calls us in the 2020s and 2030s?

It is important to note for Makgoba that, thankfully, in an era of climate change which threatens to overwhelm us all, we have in the past thirty years developed a better understanding of how abundant life for all means not just abundant life for humanity, but for all of God's creation. He notes that our theology now recognizes that our environment is not something to be exploited or ignored, but that it forms, with us, part of what Desmond Tutu called "the bundle of life". We need to keep that constantly in mind.

As I have maintained close contact with Anglican Communion leaders and in addition, I continue to teach a course at Canterbury Cathedral for seminarians and the newly ordained in the Anglican Communion, I am privy to a lot of predictions about Makgoba and his potential to break boundaries, like becoming the Archbishop of Canterbury. Of course, none of this is substantiated but demonstrates the great respect that Makgoba carries in the Anglican Communion. He offers the wisdom in our Anglican conversations that, at least in the Anglican Communion, we recognize that the era in which doing theology is dominated by western theologians is over.

Also, Makgoba recounts from his memoir, *Faith and Courage: Praying with Mandela*, how his ministry to Nelson Mandela during his last years shaped his own courage to lead through difficult times. Such inspiration provided the larger scale reference point of how the Anglican Communion's history is tied to the spread of European colonialism, to the way in which colonists wiped out the lives of indigenous peoples, and to the suffering inflicted by long-lasting practices, from slavery to denial of black franchise, to systems such as apartheid. For example, Makgoba reflects upon uncomfortable facts, such as Archbishop Thomas Secker of Canterbury's approval of reimbursements for the purchase of enslaved people to work on sugar plantations in Barbados owned by the then Society for the Propagation of the Gospel in Foreign Parts (SPG).

Makgoba's own social-political and cultural context is rooted in the northern-most province of South Africa. He comes from the Tlou clan of the Sepedi-speaking people who dominate much of the north of modern-day South Africa. The earliest surviving written records of his clan's existence show that in about 1800 they moved to a beautiful valley which came to be called Makgoba's Kloof (an approximate translation of *kloof* would be "gulf"). As you will read in Makgoba's chapter, there his great-grandfather, Kgoši (King) Mamphoku Makgoba, ruled their clan in peace until, first, the British defeated a powerful neighbor, the famed Sekhukhune of baPedi (the Pedi people), and then Dutch-speaking settlers of the Zuid-Afrikaansche Republiek defeated the British. Soon afterwards, settlers of

European heritage began to invade his family's land, either in search of gold or to peg out farms for themselves.

During the writing of his memoir, Makgoba was asked why—given the treatment of indigenous peoples across the world by people who called themselves Christian—was he a Christian? Makgoba's reply was that Christian faith begins with a young Palestinian on a donkey. Makgoba drew this phrase, and reflections on it, from the memoir written by the South African theologian, Denise Ackermann, entitled "Surprised by the Man on the Borrowed Donkey."[2] The image conjured up by Ackermann's title reveals that since Roman times we have not understood what God is up to in our world. Instead, we have imperial agendas to rule the world. Christian faith has been attached to national flags, but that is not the gospel. The good news of Christian faith is not imperialism and is not colonialism. Christian faith is about how do I love my neighbour as myself and as others.

The expected audience of this book on faith are those who resist the urge for a provincial religion, that is trapped in its own regional problems. By reading about the particularity of global spiritual leaders, a catalyst forms for many activist Christians to practice an international community who learns how to negotiate the relativity of dilemmas set forth above. Furthermore, the global world learns to anticipate the creation of new crises and is better prepared to respond. The Anglican Communion is especially suited for this task because it represents the developed

---

2. Denise Ackermann, *Surprised by the Man on the Borrowed Donkey* (Lux Verbi, 2014).

and developing world all wrapped into one, a microcosm of the world. By learning from Anglicans, hopefully others from different faiths, nationalities, and contexts can also learn about themselves. To encourage all of us to read and join in the conversations of this book and the whole Series, we pray we will also further act in ways to contribute to the consensus among socially conscious Christians that we can make this world better. In other words, the goal is to have a healthy balance between internal reflection and external witness.

PART ONE

Anglican Identity and Faith

CHAPTER ONE

Faith: A Commitment Beyond Sunday Morning

Rose Hudson-Wilkin,
Anglican Bishop of Dover

". . . . Send us out in the power of your spirit to live and work to your praise and glory."

Those who belong to the Anglican / Episcopal world will be more than familiar with the liturgical calendar, with its rhythm of morning and evening prayer as well as Holy Communion being part of our regular weekly diet of faith and hence an expression of "being church." For a large majority of people, this is where it stops. Their duty is done until they return to their place of worship a day or a week later. For many like them, faith is simply all about the activity of worship. So, the question to ask is, "what happens in the interim?" From the moment they leave that designated place of worship, what next?

As we think of faith, I cannot help but look to the words from the letter of James in the New Testament. "As the body without the spirit is dead, so faith without deeds is dead." It is not good enough to say we have faith, especially a faith which is inward-looking. For faith to be alive, it must be identified from our actions, our deeds. I therefore want to invite you to explore with me what this might mean for all of us who claim to be people of faith.

When we are baptized as children, our parents and Godparents make vows on our behalf. They affirm their belief in God in the words of the Apostle's creed. They, along with the congregation present, echo sentiments agreeing that God is adding to our numbers those who are being called into the fellowship of faith. Three prominent questions are asked: - Do you turn to Christ? Do you repent of your sins? Do you renounce evil? They respond in the affirmative: I turn to Christ. I repent of my sins. I renounce evil.

All powerful affirmations if everyone in the congregation pondered on their meaning; if in every congregation where a baptism takes place, at least 10 percent of those present were to go away and seek some meaning between the words they have heard and responded to, then we would have the start of a revival on our hands!

As a parish priest, I was always careful to point out that these statements are not just to be said once at a baptismal service and then forgotten. We daily turn to Christ. We daily say "Sorry" for the things we have done and said which we should not have done and said (including the things we should have said and done and failed to) and we daily name and renounce evil wherever we encounter evil. As the young child grows, how do we help them to engage meaningfully with these words? When do we ever sit with them and begin the process to help them in their own understanding to recognize God's call and therefore turn in the direction of that call. When do we help them to recognize why it is important to say "Sorry" and when do we help them to become courageous advocates, naming something that is wrong or evil and speaking out (or into a situation) on behalf of others.

I was always bold at baptismal services to remind the gathered congregation that the infant child will not understand the meaning of the symbolisms being used at the service; neither will they know what love, forgiveness, and compassion look like unless they see it in action within the homes of their parents and god-parents—the people who made the commitments on their behalf (and I often brought grandparents into the mix as the children are often in their homes too). It is only then that they will be able to begin to make sense of what we tell them about love, about forgiveness, and about compassion as we read the bible stories and help them make the connection with real life.

I share with baptismal families when I meet with them that my choice of godparents is not about choosing my best friends to become godparents; neither is it about selecting my favorite family member and rewarding them for their past kindness. My pattern would be to choose godparents from amongst the congregation by prayerfully discerning whom I thought would best pray for my children and help me to nurture them in the Christian faith. The faith that they are to be nurtured in must be a faith which moves beyond the confines of the worship building. This nurturing impacted on my children. I recall my daughter waking up to the news that there was a massive fire in a residential high-raised building in London. She immediately rang me up to tell me about it. When I told her that I knew about it as it began before I went to bed, she said in a rather loud voice, (as if to imply why are you still at home while this is unfolding there), "Mommy," she said, "get down there."

I attempted to explain to her the facts of parochial boundaries as set out in the Church of England. Grenfell Tower, the venue of the fire, was within a set parish boundary. A priest from another parish is not expected to just walk in and start offering pastoral care. She did not care for, and neither was she interested in, such rules of an ecclesiological nature. All she knew was that people were in serious trouble, and she wanted to see others who were able to get there and help alleviate the terrible ordeal that was being faced. The words "Mommy, get down there," still echo in my head every time I think about Grenfell Tower and the 72 people that lost their lives that night in the blaze. She had a deep conviction that faith was not just about praying. It had to be about being interested in the lives of those who are part of the community in which we live, work, and play.

Young children are introduced to the faith through baptism. The baptismal fonts in most churches are to be found near to the entrance of the church, thus symbolising baptism being the start of one's introduction to the Christian faith. The beginning of an ongoing journey. I would like to suggest that the church has a responsibility of equipping companions for those baptized to walk alongside them, nurturing them in the faith.

In my ministry as a bishop, I spend time visiting deaneries, which are geographical areas with several churches within their borders. During these visits, I always do an "In Conversation with Bishop Rose." Invariably, one of the questions I am repeatedly asked is, "What is the greatest challenge to the church at this present time?" My response is always, "A lack of confident Christians."

By confident Christians, I mean someone who knows that they believe in a God that is living, a risen God; someone who knows that they believe in a God who is interested in the ordinary lives of the people of his creation. Someone who knows that God is interested in those who are hungry and thirsty, sick and in prison, and naked, needing something as basic as to be clothed. In the story of the last judgment, those who were gathered heard the words, "I was hungry and thirsty; you gave me nothing to eat or drink. I was sick and in prison, you did not visit me. I was naked, you did not clothe me." (Matt 25:43)

The response of the gathered audience is most interesting. "We know you. If we had seen you, we would have fed you and given you something to drink. If you were sick or in prison, we would have visited you. If we saw you naked, we would have clothed you." What they failed to understand was that though they may not have seen Jesus, they saw others in a variety of predicaments and did nothing about it! So, Jesus rightly replies, "In as much as you did not help those others in need, you did not help me." (Matt 25:45)

In 1st John 4 verse 20, we read, "How can you say you love God whom you have never seen and yet do not love your sister or brother that you can see?" Those who profess a faith in God but who are unable to make that connection with their fellow human beings are missing a significant part of the puzzle. Without that missing piece, we are no more than a people with Pharisaic interests, weighed down by the letter of the law instead of the spirit of the law.

The Pharisees gathered as a brotherhood, and they were known as a Chaburah—a group of like-minded people who made a pledge in front of witnesses. They pledged to spend their lives observing every detail of the scribal law. For them, the law was the most sacred thing in the world. For them, the law was the most perfect, complete word of God containing everything one needs to know for the living of a good life! Therefore, the law was seen to hold regulations to govern every possible incident e.g. the law says, "Keep the Sabbath day holy doing no work." The Scribes, for example, set about defining what work is—listing what may or may not be done. Their whole lives were spent working out these rules and regulations. But the law given to us was not meant to become so burdensome and in effect a barrier to faith being lived.

I am always intrigued by the response Jesus gave when he was asked about what to do to inherit eternal life (Luke 10:25ff). Yes, Jesus does direct him to the law. The expert in the law quotes the summary of the Law and is reassured by Jesus that if he follows the law, all will be well. "You have answered correctly. Do this and you will live." But the expert in the law is not content and ask a further question, "Who is my neighbor?" (Luke10:29) It is then that Jesus moves him from the place of the letter of the law to the spirit and real meaning of the law. He tells him the story of the Samaritan who finds a man beaten up and left half dead on the road. Others had passed by on the same road but did nothing to assist the man.

We are even told that some of those who went by were deeply religious. No doubt they would have regarded themselves as people of faith, deeply religious men who never failed to worship—but keeping to the law. Yes, the law had something to say about cleanliness and touching this person would make them unclean. They knew the law, but they were not able to feel and show any compassion. It took a Samaritan who culturally was estranged from the Jews to recognize "the humanity of the other" and reach out with compassion to meet his needs.

I believe that some of the doctrinal fights being had in the church of varying denominations is to be likened to those pharisees who were misguided and who gave precedence to the letter of the law. All the time they were forgetting the heartbeat of the God who gave so generously to the world. "For God so loved the world that he gave his only son, that whoever believeth in him should not perish but have everlasting life." (Jn. 3:16). The heartbeat is not about following every iota of the law. It is about a love overflowing that seeks the common good for all.

Faith is more than the labels we carry. It is deep touching deep! If faith is going to matter, it must go beyond: "I am anglo-catholic, I am evangelical, I am liberal catholic, I am open evangelical, I am liberal, I am conservative evangelical" and the list goes on. We seem to invest more in these labels than in the Good News. We gather like-minded people around us and we form cliques locking others out. In the midst of this all, we forget why we worship and indeed whom we worship. We become blinded by our own desires, not the desires of our Lord and Saviour. We also become self-serving, propping up our newly built castles.

Suddenly we find ourselves behaving like guards, protecting God, choosing who can get close to God and who does not belong. In the second verse of the hymn "There's a wideness in God's mercy," we hear these words:

"But we make his love too narrow by false limits of our own; and we magnify his strictness with a zeal he would not own. For the love of God is broader than the measure of our mind, and the heart of the eternal is most wonderfully kind." As I read and re-read scripture, I find nothing there where God ask for our protection.

After all, He is God. As a child in Sunday school, I used to sing "My God is so big, so strong and so mighty, there's nothing my God cannot do. The mountains are his, the valleys are his, the stars are his handiworks too. . . ." In our desire to prove that we have the answer, we have domesticated God, made him too small and enlarged ourselves and our organizations at the expense of the gospel. All the time we are doing this, we are not giving time to exploring how faith is to be lived in our communities so that others of no faith may catch a glimpse of the glory of God.

Let me share the story of Dennis Bailey, who lived faith. He was not a celebrity, just an ordinary man who came to England from St Lucia. One can imagine the excitement on this young man's face on his arrival in England, carrying the dreams and hopes of the many left behind. I met him shortly after I moved to Hackney in Northeast London. He worshipped at his beloved St Peter de Beauvoir Church where he assisted as a sacristan, including cleaning the silver and the brass. Soon after I moved to the neighbouring parish, he would come on to All Saints where I served at the end of his service in St Peters church.

He was a real gentleman, quietly spoken, who never had the opportunity for an academic education but willingly allowed life to be his teacher. Midweek, he shared his best gift. He would go up to the hospital during visiting hours and whichever bed had no visitor, he would go and talk with them. "I was sick and in prison and you visited me. . ." He lived those words in the post-communion prayer, "Send us out in the power of your Spirit to live and work to your praise and glory." St Peter was not just the place where he worshipped, but the place where his faith equipped him as he encountered life and he was able to make the connection between faith and works.

As I write, Britain is in the throes of its national election. Already there is much anxiety around issues of immigration. The public are being told that the woes they are experiencing, such as not being able to access a dentist or see a doctor, not being able to get access to decent housing, is because of the country being overcrowded with both legal and illegal immigrants. Sadly, there are many in the country who believe this kind of rhetoric. They have come to believe that the economic downturn that is impacting on them personally is because of immigrants coming to the country.

Politicians pushing the immigration button are being irresponsible. They are encouraging "othering" in our communities; a process whereby we cast blame, usually on a group of people who we tell ourselves are not like us. In many of our communities, we seek out people who come to our country seeking to flourish and build a better life for themselves and their families. So, the people who are already most vulnerable carry the brunt of society's corrupt propaganda.

Many politicians, including some of faith, have been silent. They appear to be afraid to speak out in case they lose the popular vote. We see this silence, too, in the failure of Christian politicians and citizens to name the storming of Capital Hill and those who colluded with it as wrong. Their silence is most disappointing. We need prophetic voices—"The voice of one crying in the wilderness," voices that are willing to stand with those who are disenfranchised, voices willing to challenge the going narrative with a more reflective tone that is covered in prayer.

People of faith must be the ones to remind the world, the communities of which we are a part, that we are part of the one human race and that we are "our brother's keeper." People of faith must remind themselves and the world that in Christ "There is neither Jew nor Greek, there is neither slave nor free, there is neither male nor female; for you are all one in Christ Jesus." (Gal.3:28)

If we are all one, then we have a responsibility to compassionately respond to the needs of the others. It is not enough to join in with the cries of "too many immigrants coming to our country." We must ask instead, "Why are people leaving their homes, is it war, climate change, unscrupulous leaders caring only about power and money, is it famine?" There is indeed a desperate need for the international community to begin to address the movements of people across the world. This cannot be left alone for right wing extremist to make their case. People of faith need to speak up on behalf of the men, women, and children who are most vulnerable in our world and in our communities.

Richer countries in the West, who have taken much from the countries where people are migrating from in the name of empire and colonialism, can no longer say, "This has nothing to do with me." They must get around the table and work with these countries. This should mean investing in those countries, not selling weapons to unscrupulous leaders of countries, not cutting international aid. They must invest in diplomacy, the kind of diplomacy that enables conflict resolution across the world.

I recently attended the launch at Lambeth Palace of a program referred to as "The Difference." At the heart of this program is an explicit desire to work with young people, enabling them to reimagine the kind of society they want to live in. The program seeks to empower them, to help them recognize that they have it within them to make a difference and to be the change they want to see. To do this, they are equipped to be curious and present in their surroundings, thus creating that which they have reimagined. They spend time engaging in "meaningful dialogue, practical exercises and reflective activities." This program emphasizes the reality that the work of peace and reconciliation begins with intentionality.

So much of our time and that of many governments is given to addressing the presenting issues. Issues such as mass migration, poverty, breakdown of relationships, conflict, wars, and the abuse of women and girls. If we are serious about wanting to see change, creating a world where there is love and respect, a world where people can experience abundant life as God intended for all his children ("*I am come that they may have life and have it more abundantly.*" John 10:10), then we must invest in the work of creating a positive change. I am excited that "The Difference" program is making it possible for young people—the next generation—to be part of the solution now and not wait until the world thinks they have come of age according to some artificial standard set by our society.

All people of faith must be prepared to engage in these debates, always ensuring that they create the change they want to see. People of faith are needed to remind the world that the Old and New Testament speaks much about the movement of peoples across the world. People will move to less hostile environments in order to feel safe or to feed themselves and their families. No one stays put with bombs raining down on them.

I feel a deep sense of compulsion to speak out into this heated debate around immigration. Several of our politicians have placed migration at the heart of their campaign. The rhetoric being bandied around is negative and could be described as "the othering of people" who do not look like us or sound like us. Faith demands that we challenge this narrative and do all we can to work for a world where all God's people can live with dignity and respect.

The kind of human destruction that we have seen unfolding before our very eyes in Israel and Gaza, the Sudan, Myanmar, Ukraine, and especially through social media, highlights a world of "them and us." It is only in a world where I am human and you are less than human, that I can afford to brutally destroy you because you are not like me. It is only in a world where I do not recognize your humanity that I can fail to show compassion as I see women and children walking for days to escape the violence of war or to escape poverty while we stand by and look disinterested. Contrast this with the story of the feeding of the five thousand. When the disciples told Jesus that the gathered crowd was not his problem, that he had done his bit, we are told that "Jesus had compassion." He was concerned that they were hungry and he did not want them to faint on the journey home. (Mark 6:30–44)

What a difference it would make if we were to think of helping to meet each other's needs; if we were to recognize that my well-being is dependent on your well-being. What a difference it would make if all those professing faith were to recognize that we all share a common humanity and that the same kind of success we want for ourselves and our families is the same thing that is required by another who may have been born in another country thousands of miles away.

I believe politicians in the West have a responsibility not only to ensure that there is good governance in their country, but that they have a responsibility to work for a world where there can be enough food for all and where you're not having to watch your child die because there is no health care, or see your child abused simply because she happens to have been born a girl. Politicians in the West have a responsibility to work for a world where all children, irrespective of where they were born, have access to a good education; a world where young women in particular do not need to live in fear.

If we can take time to read from the 1st chapter in the book of Ruth in the Old Testament, we will find a holistic picture which reflects a community caring for those most vulnerable. How easy it would have been for Ruth, the young daughter-in-law, to think only of herself, the possibility of getting re-married and starting a new life after the death of her husband. But both women are thinking of each other. On Ruth's part, she is thinking, "what kind of life will my mother-in-law have on her own?" On

Naomi's part, she is thinking, "Ruth and Orpah must go back to their parents in order to start a new life." Ruth understands however, that to make a success of the future without their husbands, they will need to work together. "Intreat me not to leave thee or from following after thee, for wither thou goest, I will go; thy people shall be my people and thy God, my God." [Ruth 1:16–17]

In this brand-new world, Ruth could have been preyed upon by the young men while they were out reaping the crop. But they were told in no uncertain terms that this would not be acceptable. Someone in authority must step up to the plate and be the voice of decency, be the voice of justice and truth. We cannot continue to give tacit agreement to a "Them and Us." Real faith must witness to the one human family. As followers of Christ, it is the mission of all, regardless of color, creed, or culture to be engaged in building bridges, not putting up walls. It is about the Kingdom of God which unites, not divides the human family. It is about reaching out to those who are poor, whether they are visibly in front of your very eyes or they are across the seas.

A significant part of my ministry is spent visiting with schools both primary and secondary. The primary children are always keen to ask me what I enjoy most about being a bishop. I tell them that being with children and young people is a great treat for me. Invariably, another child in the class will always ask me, "What do you not enjoy about being a bishop?" I say to them, "Do you really want to know?" By now their little heads are bobbing up and down, so I give in and say, "Adults behaving like children."

I go on to tell them that when they are out at playtime and they fall out with their friends, usually before they are back in their classes, they have made up. "Not so, with the adults, they continue to hold a grudge." The children do find this amusing, but behind this is a serious thought. We must always be ready to forgive and to make sure that the words we speak from our lips is being emanated from a good place, from our hearts.

This faith we profess is not a touchy-feely thing that we put on display when we feel like it. Neither is it private or a secret affair. Faith is a gift that when received is to be rooted in the scriptures, giving us a firm foundation from which to grow shoots of life. While taking questions from a group of 11-year-olds, I was asked which I would choose, Good Friday or Easter. I shared with them why I was choosing Good Friday. If there was no Good Friday, then there would have been no Easter Day.

Thinking of Good Friday, I am reminded that with faith, we cannot be bystanders. On the first Good Friday, Simon of Cyrene was simply being a bystander going about his own business and perhaps pausing to see what was happening. He may have been a bystander but was destined not to be an anonymous one. He was compelled by the soldiers to carry the cross, (no doubt giving Jesus some well-deserved respite).

I am left to wonder what it was that drew Simon of Cyrene into the path of the drama that was unfolding that day. Was it empathy that drew him to watch, to feel, and maybe even to mourn. I want to suggest that as people of faith, compassion ought to be our driver. That which enables us not just to walk on by, but to pause and feel with the downtrodden and those who society pushes to the edge of society. We need to be a community that is prepared to weep and wail for the atrocities of gun and knife crime; for the devastation in Sudan, Syria, Palestine and Israel, the ongoing human trafficking across the world, the plight of the Rohingya people in Myanmar, the gang warfare in parts of South America, and the ill-treatment of women and girls around the world and for all injustices across the planet.

We need to pattern our Lord who stands in the midst of those who are suffering and weep as he wept at the pain of loss for his friends. From the flowing tears comes love and forgiveness. On the cross, our Lord cried out, "Father forgive them, for they do not know what they are doing." There is some truth in the words "they do not know what they are doing." We too do not always know what we are doing. We often seek to remain in a state of anonymity, afraid of being propelled to the place of deep emotions; afraid of not being in control.

And yet it is God who ultimately is in control. The God "who knows our needs before we ask. . . ." (a prayer in our Anglican liturgy). The prayer continues, "help us to ask only what accords to your will; and the good things which we dare not, or in our blindness cannot ask, grant us for the sake of your Son, Jesus Christ our Lord."

I recalled once, at a time of feeling troubled, reaching for the bible. It fell open at Leviticus 19. In the second verse, I read the words, "Be holy as I am holy." I sighed heavily as I was expecting to go through chapter after chapter, giving instructions of what kind of work to be engaged in to achieve holiness. Instead, I find words which speaks into how we treat others: our parents; how we treat the poor and the alien; how we treat our neighbor, those who work for us; how we treat those with disability and the need to respect the elderly.

The mark of holiness expressed through faith is not about the personal morality of those who claim to profess faith. God is not interested in our personal morality. Neither is God interested in our numerous man-made rituals that we have created and pretended that they are the most important thing ever. Holiness is described for us as a mark of how we advocate for those in need of care.

In the Acts of the Apostles, we further learn that "spiritual virtues" was not the only thing that contributed to the growth of the early church. Instead, the growth that was being experienced was due to the wider needs of all the believers being taken care of (Acts 4:32–36), "No one was in need." This is faith beyond the bounds of religiosity that many would have locked up within the doors of our churches and cathedrals.

In 1st and 2nd Timothy, it is impressed upon us to pray for our governments. In 1 Timothy 2:1–2, we read, "I urge, then, first of all, that petitions, prayers, intercession and thanksgiving be made for Kings and all those in authority, that we may live peaceful and quiet lives in all godliness and holiness." Again we see faith as something expressed as a natural outworking of our spiritual lives.

In South Africa, during the height of the apartheid movement, it was the men and women of faith, of which Archbishop Desmond Tutu was most prominent. He was to be heard speaking out about the injustices of apartheid and could be seen at the front of marches calling for freedom. The words of Isaiah handed to Jesus in the temple would have been real to Archbishop Tutu and an encouragement to their protest. "The Spirit of the Lord is on me, because he has anointed me to preach good news to the poor. He has sent me to proclaim freedom for the prisoners and recovery of sight to the blind, to release the oppressed, to proclaim the year of the Lord's favor." (Luke 4:18–19)

This passage of scripture carries great significance for me too. It was part of my call to ministry. One that I continue to hold dear, knowing that my call is to a life of proclamation of God's Good News in Christ expressed in action. It speaks to me of striving to meet every human as we "proclaim the year of the Lord's favor."

Archbishop Tutu made popular the word UBUNTU. This is a word from the Xhosa language. It means, "I am because you are." It is an ancient African word meaning "humanity for others." It believes that there is a special bond that connects us together as one human race. If we believe this, then this ought to be seen in the relationship we share with one another.

In the past, when I served as a parish priest, I was asked during a discussion sermon the following question, "Are our churches closing because we see mosques and temples being built here in England?" I responded with an emphatic "No, our churches are closing because those of us who profess faith are failing to live that faith."

In scripture so much is spoken of about love, but in many of our churches we practice the very opposite. Every time I receive a letter that says, "I am not speaking to my priest, or fellow Churchwarden," my heart is broken. I believe that this breaks the heart of our Lord too. We take offense so easily— it is almost as if we are looking for something to be offended by and like a disease it is quickly spread throughout the community, planting seeds of distrust and deepening the enmity.

I am reminded of the story of the Syro-Phoenecian woman (Mark 7:24–30). She begged for her daughter to be healed. Jesus responds to her saying, "Let the children be fed first, for it is not fair to take the children's food and throw it to the dogs." She replies to Jesus, "Sir, even the dogs under the table eat the children's crumbs." I remember feeling deeply uncomfortable about this exchange between Jesus and this mother. What could Jesus be thinking by adding to the distress of this poor woman, clearly in pain at her daughter's illness. He appears to be likening her daughter to a dog! Already I can feel myself being cross with Jesus on her behalf.

What is deeply beautiful about this story told in the gospel of Mark is that this woman has no time to take offense, her only concern is her daughter's well-being. She is not looking for a reason to have a fight with Jesus. In her response suggesting that the dogs sometime eat the crumbs which fall from the table, she is clearly saying, "I will be content with the crumbs if that is what is going to make my daughter well again." In this woman's response, we capture something of her faith. She was not giving up. She was confidently hanging on: "I'll have the crumbs, if that's all that is coming my way."

It is possible that Jesus was caught off guard, wanting a bit of downtime when he would "just be," and not doing or performing any miracles. This mother with a need noticed Jesus. She was curious because she had heard much about him. She may have wondered; might he be able to heal her daughter? Her curiosity led her not only to listen but get behind the words that Jesus was speaking. No wonder she was not angry with Jesus' outburst. Not so with us. We rarely listen to each other. We seem ready to pounce, to take offense. What are we afraid of? Our fears and insecurities prevent us from having a deeper faith experience.

We rarely listen to God, too, because we are so sure we already know the answers long before the questions are even asked. We fail to nurture the kind of curiosity that enables us to truly listen to each other's perspective and therefore truly encounter the other. Jesus chooses to remain present with her, as he did similarly with the woman at the well in John 4. It is vitally important for the people of God to seek to be incarnationally present with those around us. Those who are suffering, those who are marginalized, and including those whom we do not agree with.

Staying "present" enables us to be of service to those on the edges as well as those in the center; the known and the unknown. This mother stayed present and engaged, and as a result both she and her daughter received the healing and wholeness they sought. This woman, no doubt seen by some as an outsider, is recognized and valued by God. One suspects that some would have her be silent, after all "she is a woman." Our Lord is not afraid for her voice to be heard, for her to be visible and engaged in his presence. Jesus did not object to her answering back, going "toe to toe" with him!

This woman's story is one of confident hope, and ultimately of faith. She was a good example of walking by faith and not by sight. Her response models something of what it means to be part of God's mission that we are called to be a part of, as God's

Church for God's World. I wonder how as people of faith we might together re-imagine the kind of transformation that this kind of response can bring about amongst the people of God locally, nationally and internationally, holding together as one in all our diversities.

Faith ought to undergird all that we are in all the circumstances that we find ourselves in. When faith is present, we are better able to face each day, whatever the obstacles in our way. I want to suggest, however, that instead of living into our faith we make the mistake of busying ourselves, trying to usurp God's role. In Mark's gospel Jesus shares this with his listeners: "The kingdom of God is as if a man should scatter seed on the ground. He sleeps and rises night and day, and the seed sprouts and grows; he knows not how. The earth produces by itself, first the blade, then the ear, then the full grain in the ear." (Mark 4:26–33)

In this story, Jesus reminds his listeners that their responsibility lies in their ability to faithfully plant seeds and in effect to scatter them generously. So, no planning for some neat rows as we often find in an orchard or in a vineyard. We are just to get out there and be generous with whatever resources we find ourselves with. Scatter them far and wide and let God do the rest. But again, only when there is faith will we be able to let go, trusting that God will rightly do His part. According to Mark, the man scatters the seeds and then falls asleep night after night, "He sleeps and rises night and day, and the seeds sprouts and grows; he knows not how." What an expression of faith and trust in God! He can see the growth day after day; Yes, he scattered the seeds but the growth, "He knows not how." Don't look at him, this is God's doing. He didn't do it.

The more we recognize that it is not about our power or our might, that it is not up to us to fix things, then it becomes more possible for us to relax into trusting God and living out faith. To truly live as Christians, faith must be our foundation. In Matthew's gospel, the disciples wanted to know how it is they could not heal the boy with the demon who was presented to them by the boy's father. Jesus' response to them was, "Because you have so little faith." But Jesus went on to say to them, "If you have faith as a mustard seed...nothing will be impossible for you."

I am encouraged by the thought that we are not expected to compare the degree of our faith with others. This would be counter-productive. Jesus' use of the mustard seed is to let us know that however little our faith is, we are to put it into action, trusting God to do his part. We all know how small the mustard seed is, but when planted, "We know not how" it grew into an amazingly large tree. We are reminded by this story that with a small start, big things can happen.

If we are going to make a difference, I believe that we will need to be intentional in our generosity in scattering the seeds of God's love, of being God's hands, his feet and his voice. We will need to walk in the footsteps of our Lord, deepening our trust in God and then living out the faith in the communities where we live and work. From the mustard seeds that we plant, in faith we will see the trees growing because we will exhibit that trust in our God to do his part.

At the present moment, it feels like the church is about to be deeper engulfed in "navel gazing," arguing amongst ourselves as to whose beliefs are more orthodox than the other. We seem to be sharpening our tools ready for conflict, ready indeed for battle. The threatening emails are flying fast, making demands of new provinces, new training establishments and the need for these to have a "pure" space which is "sin free and orthodox!"

Well, I do not know that space and neither do I want to be a part of that space. I want my feet to be on the ground as Jesus' were—walking and serving amongst those whom society pushed aside as not being good enough or holy enough. I call to mind what Jesus had to say about the Pharisees—those whom Jesus referred to as "hypocrites and whitewashed sepulchres." He also said that they were giving people heavy burdens to carry. Their zeal for faithfulness was mostly about outward appearances; in focusing on the minutia, they were losing sight of the message of love, forgiveness, grace, and compassion.

Our focus on faith must surely remind us that the core of our message should be about the Kingdom of God, not in some far away distant place and time but right now and right here in our midst. God becoming human and dwelling in our midst and teaching us how to live and be with one another. Faith indeed begins with Love. Not our love but with God who loved us first ("in that while we were yet sinners, Christ died for us"). We pattern that love as we seek to proclaim the message of His Good News in words and deeds. In the words of Paul, "Three things will last forever—faith, hope and love—and the greatest of these is love." (1 Cor. 13:13)

CHAPTER TWO

A New Global Paradigm: the Anglican Communion in Historical Perspective[1]

The Revd. Canon Dr. Stephen Spencer,
Anglican Communion Office, London

What is the Anglican Communion? The origins of the term begin to answer the question, especially in the way it grew out of the missionary movement. By the early nineteenth century, there was widespread awareness that there were a number of different Anglican churches, not just one Church of England, spread across the world. When the British Parliament passed the Bishops of Foreign Countries Act in 1841, legal permission was granted for the Church of England to consecrate a bishop for a foreign country who need not be a subject of the British crown nor take the oaths of allegiance to the monarch. This allowed the creation of missionary bishops outside of Britain and its dependencies, leading to thirty-three new overseas bishops being put in place by 1860. This made it clear that Anglicanism was now a global phenomenon. As Ephraim Radner put it,

---

1. Some of the content of this article is a revised version of content in Stephen Spencer and Joseph Galgalo, 2023, "Anglican Theology," *Encyclopedia of Theology*, St Andrew's University, www.saet.ac.uk/Christianity/AnglicanTheology.

Finally, by the mid-nineteenth century, the actual phrase "Anglican Communion" emerged from a very specific missionary context: the Jubilee Anniversary of the Society for the Propagation of the Gospel (SPG), which had been a leader, despite all its foibles, in the Anglican spread of the Gospel. There *is* a communion of Anglican churches, observers noted, precisely as it is the embodied expression of the missionary thrust of Anglicans to plant the Gospel in all places. (Radner 2017,133)

Since then, of course, the dioceses and provinces of the Anglican Communion have grown to a much greater extent and now include over 40 autonomous churches/provinces[2] around the world with an estimated membership of around 85 million.

But with this spread of Anglican churches across the globe, there arose the question of how authority was to be exercised across jurisdictions. Was the classical Anglican paradigm of authority coming top-down from the English monarch as "Supreme Governor" to hold sway?[3] Before 1841, with two exceptions, this the case, because from 1634, the Bishop of

---

2. These terms will be used interchangeably in this chapter even though some autonomous Anglican churches include a number of provinces within their territories.

3. As in "His Majesty's Declaration" introducing the Articles of Religion in the Book of Common Prayer 1662: "BEING by God's Ordinance, according to Our just Title, Defender of the Faith, and Supreme Governor of the Church, within these Our Dominions, We hold it most agreeable to this Our Kingly Office, and Our own religious Zeal, to conserve and maintain the Church committed to Our Charge, in Unity of true Religion, and in the Bond of Peace; and not to suffer unnecessary Disputations, Altercations, or Questions to be raised, which may nourish Faction both in the Church and Commonwealth."

London, who was appointed by the crown, was given episcopal oversight of "English congregations gathering abroad and to clergy ministering to them."[4] But as more and more bishops were established after 1841, the question of international structure and how a common discipline was to be enforced became ever more urgent.

This reached a crisis point in the 1860's, with division across provinces over whether to recognize biblical criticism, especially between Bishop Colenso of Natal in South Africa and his critics. The Archbishop of Canterbury, Charles Longley, prompted by Canadian bishops, decided to call a conference of all bishops in 1867. It met at the archbishop's main residence, Lambeth Palace in London, which gave its name to the conference, with seventy-six bishops attending. It was, however, boycotted by the Archbishop of York, supported by the bishops of Durham, Carlisle, and Ripon, who refused to attend because they feared the conference would weaken the link between the Church of England and the British state (Jacob 1997, 163). Longley was not deterred and his invitation letter indicates a positive purpose for the conference, with its statement that the gathering was to be for "the maintenance of greater union in our missionary work and to increased intercommunion among ourselves" (Avis and Guyer 2017, 298). The building of unity across difference, especially for mission, then, was to be its primary purpose. Longley also made it clear the meeting would not be a synod

---

4. The exceptions were the Scottish Episcopal Church, retaining Anglican orders but without the established status of the Church of England, this passing to the Presbyterian Church of Scotland, and the Episcopal Church, separated from the Church of England at the American War of Independence.

for the governing of provinces but a consultative and fraternal meeting. There would be no issuing of directives and regulations by a mother church to its daughter churches, as it were.

This invitation can therefore be seen as one of the first official expressions of a new and emerging paradigm of Anglican life across the world, one in which a top-down hierarchical authority, whether of the authority of the British monarch or the Archbishop of Canterbury or the Church of England in general, would be replaced by a very different authority structure, one of a fraternity of equal churches in which authority comes from the finding of consensus. Such a structure and its very different habitus[5] implies a different perspective on how the Anglican Communion is conceived, structured, and how constituent parts relate to each other. A pyramidal organization is turned on its head and a figure like the Archbishop of Canterbury no longer acts in authority *over* the other bishops but becomes a facilitator of consultation in which all engage as equal partners. This has implications for every area of church life, from worship through to mission and discipleship. This can appropriately be described as a new and emerging paradigm of the Anglican Communion.

Since then, the Lambeth Conference has met fifteen times, most recently in 2022, and considered an increasingly wide range of questions, seeking consensus about them among the bishops. As a result of this consultation, there have been some significant ecclesiological developments, some of which will be considered below. They began with the conference of 1888 adopting the

---

5. All the norms, values, attitudes, and behaviours that are fostered by a particular social structure.

Chicago Quadrilateral, setting out core tenets of church doctrine. The conference of 1908 was notable for affirming aspects of social Christianity. The conference of 1920 issued an historic appeal for the unity of all Christians. The conference of 1930 was important for its definition of the Anglican Communion and for recognizing that artificial contraception may sometimes be right, this being extended in 1958 to viewing family planning as "a positive choice before God" (Sedgwick 2020).

One of the reports for the conference of 1948 produced a finely nuanced description of how authority in Anglicanism is not centralized through a hierarchical structure but dispersed, finding unity over time through the *consensus fidelium* (Report IV, Anglican Communion 1948). The conference of 1968 recommended the creation of a permanent diaconate open to both women and men, allowing women to preach, baptize, and lead worship (Methuen 2020). The conference of 1988 launched a "Decade of Evangelism" for the Communion in the 1990s. It also recognized that polygamists who come to faith should be allowed to be baptized, showing a growing recognition of the place of indigenous culture in the lives of Anglicans (Methuen 2020).

The 1998 conference promoted and supported the forming of companionship links across the dioceses of the Communion. But it also, famously, passed Resolution 1.10, which among other clauses rejected homosexual practice "as incompatible with Scripture" and advised against "the legitimizing or blessing of same sex unions nor ordaining those involved in same gender unions." This was passed in the face of strong opposition from a minority of bishops and is an atypical resolution for Lambeth conferences in that it "did not seem designed to seek the greatest possible degree of consensus and unity" (Zink 2017). It shows the emergence of resistance to the new paradigm, resistance that throws into relief the dominance of the new paradigm at Lambeth. But we will see this resistance growing in the new century.

A related development, but to do with the internal governing of provinces, comes from Aotearoa New Zealand. In the mid-nineteenth century, the Anglican Church here was known as the Church of England in New Zealand and by 1858 it had become the largest religious denomination with more than half the population being Anglican. This made its primate, Archbishop George Selwyn, grapple with how it was to be governed. It was not an established church, as in England, but one among others, and so creativity was needed. Consultation over a constitution took fifteen years and Selwyn worked for a diocese inclusive of Māori and Pakeha [White people]. His "genius lay in providing, in 1857, the New Zealand church with a constitution which gave the church a legal independence from the Church of England." (Ward 2006, 289) This involved the church having a legislative general synod of three distinct orders, of bishops, clergy and laity who voted separately on church matters, ensuring that each group had an equal voice.

Dioceses were also to have diocesan synods, who would nominate a new bishop when one was needed. The general synod would not be allowed to alter the authorized version of the Bible, the Book of Common Prayer or the Article of Religion, but it could function independently of the State. This constitution would come to serve as a model for other provinces, in South Africa, the West Indies, Japan and Canada and would influence the Church of Ireland:

Selwyn during these years had taken a very important step towards creating a federation of interdependent Anglican provinces. In so doing he had drawn importantly on the example of the PECUSA [the American Episcopal Church], and had helped to cement their example into the Anglican tradition (Jacob 1997, 142–3).

But as churches grew and spread from continent to continent, and became more diverse in the ways they expressed their faith, another question became more and more pressing: what do they hold in common? For if churches simply develop in different directions and gradually separate from each other, it makes little sense to look for a new overarching paradigm. One influential answer has been to point to a shared and agreed core of texts and practices. William Reed Huntington (1838–1909), an American Episcopal priest from Massachusetts, suggested this in his description of there being four signs or elements common to Protestant churches. These were the "Holy Scriptures, as the Word of God;" "the Primitive Creeds as the Rule of Faith;" "the two Sacraments ordained by Christ himself;" and "the Episcopate as the keystone of governmental unity" (Huntington in Avis and Guyer 2017, 91).

Huntington believed these four common elements are found in the mainline denominations and could form the basis of "Home Reunion" with them. The House of Bishops of the General Convention of the Episcopal Church then adopted Huntington's four points at its meeting in Chicago in 1886, followed by the bishops at the third Lambeth Conference in

1888, who resolved to adopt this "quadrilateral" (later known as the Chicago Quadrilateral) on behalf of the Anglican Communion as a whole. In Resolution 11, the Lambeth bishops resolved that in the opinion of this Conference the following Articles supply a basis on which approach may be by God's blessing made towards Home Reunion:

(a) The Holy Scriptures of the Old and New Testaments, as "containing all things necessary to salvation" [Article VI], and as being the rule and ultimate standard of faith.

(b) The Apostles' Creed, as the Baptismal Symbol; and the Nicene Creed, as the sufficient statement of the Christian faith.

(c) The two Sacraments ordained by Christ Himself—Baptism and the Supper of the Lord—ministered with unfailing use of Christ's words of Institution, and of the elements ordained by Him.

(d) The Historic Episcopate, locally adapted in the methods of its administration to the varying needs of the nations and peoples called of God into the Unity of His Church (Anglican Communion 1888).

A foundation was therefore laid for all mainline churches to recognize and affirm these four points within their own life, thus establishing common ground for moving towards unity. But in the twentieth century, this Quadrilateral has also come to be seen as defining a common core of Anglican theology and practice, an Anglican watermark, as it were, that runs through all the provinces of the Anglican Communion, more important than ever as they become increasingly diverse in the way they understand and practice their faith. This Quadrilateral is significant because it makes no reference to the see of Canterbury let alone the Church of England, showing that provinces could be fully Anglican whatever their relationship with Canterbury. In other words, it was being implied that they were now "sister churches" rather than a "parent with daughter churches," another important facet of the emergence of the new paradigm.

However, on occasions, the older Canterbury-centered paradigm has been reasserted. This was the case with a description of the Communion produced by the Lambeth Conference of 1930. In Resolution 49, the Communion is described as a fellowship, within the one holy catholic and apostolic church, of those duly constituted dioceses, provinces or regional churches in communion with the see of Canterbury (Anglican Communion 1930).

While this is clear that the Anglican Communion is only part of the Church of God and therefore never complete within itself, which shows the necessity of ecumenism, it also asserted that for a church to belong to the Communion it must be in communion with the see of Canterbury (i.e. be able to share Holy Communion with the Archbishop of Canterbury and the people of his diocese). This provided a defining boundary for working out those who belonged and those who did not. This in turn gave significant central authority to the Archbishop of Canterbury and his diocese, who could decide whom they were in communion with and whom not. The description went on to assert, however, that member churches are "bound together not by a central legislative and executive authority, but by mutual loyalty sustained through the common counsel of the Bishops in conference" (Anglican Communion 1930). This latter clause is in tension with the former, suggesting an uneasy presence of the different paradigms within the one description.

The increasing influence of the new paradigm is more clearly demonstrated by the growing ecumenical commitment of Anglicans, from the Lambeth Conference of 1920 onwards. This followed the traumas and devastation of the First World War and came out of a widespread desire to bring reconciliation to the world. It is the moment when the ecumenical calling of Anglicanism received its definitive expression, launching the involvement of the Anglican Communion in the ecumenical movement of the twentieth century. It took place in the groundbreaking and influential "Appeal to All Christian People," a call for Christian unity which offered a "new outlook" for "a new age." It is not only a defining moment for Anglican ecumenism but for the theological nature of Anglicanism itself. The appeal appeared in Resolution 9 on the "Reunion of Christendom." It was by far the longest of the resolutions. The opening paragraph makes some resounding affirmations:

We, Archbishops, Bishops Metropolitan, and other Bishops of the Holy Catholic Church in full communion with the Church of England [. . .] acknowledge all those who believe in our Lord Jesus Christ, and have been baptized into the name of the Holy Trinity, as sharing with us membership in the universal Church of Christ which is his Body. We believe that the Holy Spirit has called us in a very solemn and special manner to associate ourselves in penitence and prayer with all those who deplore the divisions of Christian people, and are inspired by the vision and hope of a visible unity of the whole Church (Anglican Communion 1920).

After the mutual suspicion and competitiveness of churches in previous centuries, these are broad and generous affirmations. The first section then sets out the groundwork to this, providing an inclusive definition of the nature of the catholic church, one which importantly sees it not as an institution existing for its own sake but for "the world-wide service of the Kingdom of God" (Ibid., section I), a missionary purpose. It then laments the divisions between the historic churches of east and west, and of the Protestant denominations, "each one keeping to itself gifts that rightly belong to the whole fellowship" (Ibid., section II). This broken fellowship is contrary to God's will: "The time has come, we believe, for all the separated groups of Christians to agree in forgetting the things which are behind and reaching out towards the goal of a reunited Catholic Church" (Ibid., section IV).

The appeal, however, is not for the church to become uniform. Churches "would retain much that has long been distinctive in their methods of worship and service. It is through a rich diversity of life and devotion that the unity of the whole fellowship will be fulfilled." (Ibid., section IV) Is this not a clear expression of the new paradigm, this time within an ecumenical context, of churches forming a fraternity of different yet equal partners in which authority comes from the finding of consensus?

But what is this consensus that will unite the churches? The bishops recognize the existence of a core of faith and practice across traditions, quoting the Chicago-Lambeth Quadrilateral of 1888, which, as we have seen, defines this core as being the scriptures, the creeds, the sacraments, and the apostolic ministry received from Christ. The Appeal also re-orientates Anglican theology from describing itself as "Protestant" to describing itself as "Catholic," albeit a form of catholicism that includes not just Roman Catholics and Orthodox but any "who believe in our Lord Jesus Christ, and have been baptized into the name of the Holy Trinity" (Chapman 2020).

The twentieth century provides some striking examples of this ecumenical consensus becoming a reality in some parts of the world, especially among the Protestant churches of the Indian sub-continent, with the creation of the Church of South India in 1947, which united Presbyterian, Congregational, Baptist, Methodist and Anglican churches to become the second largest church in India after the Roman Catholic Church. This was followed in 1970 by the creation of the Church of North India, then the Church of Pakistan, which also included Lutherans, and in 1974 by the Church of Bangladesh.

Such drawing closer to other churches has been symbolized by meetings of Archbishops of Canterbury with church leaders around the world, including the first meeting of an Archbishop of Canterbury with the Pope (Archbishop Geoffrey Fisher and Pope John XXIII in 1960). Archbishop Michael Ramsey met with the Orthodox patriarchs of Constantinople and Moscow, as well as with Pope Paul VI, and served as president of the World Council of Churches (WCC) between 1961 and 1968, and Archbishop

Robert Runcie welcomed Pope John Paul II to Canterbury Cathedral in 1982, where on pilgrimage together at St Thomas Becket's tomb, they prayed and renewed their commitment to "a common witness to the Gospel" (IARCCUM 2006, 4), a powerful expression of unity in mission across difference in structures.

Arising out of all this, member churches of the Anglican Communion have entered into a range of rich and productive dialogues with other churches (Anglican Communion 2019). This has resulted in the production of statements, based on the fraternity and consensus of the participants, that have contributed significantly to Anglican self-understanding as well ecumenical understanding. Noteworthy are,

- World Council of Churches, *Baptism, Eucharist, and Ministry*, 1982, the Lima Statement, laying down a basis for mutual recognition of each other's sacraments and ministry. The Anglican theologian Mary Tanner, then working for the World Council of Churches, was a significant contributor to this.

- Anglican and Roman Catholic International Commission I, *Final Report*, 1981. This concise report showed the two Communions looking behind the divisions of the Reformation era, finding common theological ground and new ways to describe it. The Anglican theologian Henry Chadwick was a key contributor to this influential landmark of serious ecumenical research.

- Anglican and Roman Catholic International Commission II, *Church as Communion*, 1990, which showed both

Communions embracing the ecumenical consensus about *koinonia* as a defining concept of the Church in the New Testament. This has had major ecumenical implications, leading to widespread recognition of the diocese as the basic unit of the Church. It demonstrated remarkable convergence of the thinking of J. M. R. Tillard on the Roman Catholic side and Oliver O'Donovan and Henry Chadwick on the Anglican side.

- Anglican Communion, *The Virginia Report*, 1997, written largely as a reception of the work of ARCIC I and II, it was also offered to help guide the Anglican Communion through its own differences on authority, order, structure, and decision-making, with an eye to the wider Christian context.

- Anglican Communion, *The Anglican Covenant* of 2009 affirmed what had already been agreed (such as the Quadrilateral and 1920 Appeal) and was striking for its presentation of ecumenism as the particular charism and vocation of Anglicanism. It was also written with an eye to other churches and communions joining covenanted churches as well. While the proposal of a covenant did not receive enough assent from member churches to become an ongoing part of Anglican Communion life, the text as a whole stands as a recent fruit of churches consulting in fraternity and finding consensus on a broad swathe of Anglican ecclesiology.

The new paradigm under pressure

Local diversities and the formation of national churches saw the growth of provinces, archdioceses, and metropolitan jurisdictions to meet emerging organizational needs (Ross 2020). Over time, provincial or national churches have continued to participate in the life of the global communion, embracing the need for interdependence but without relinquishing autonomy and the exercise of dispersed authority or jurisdictional independence. But local autonomy, which has become the hallmark of Anglican ecclesiology, has sometimes led to real difficulties. Without mechanisms for a central intervention, from Canterbury or the Primates collectively or any other body, it has sometimes been impossible to resolve matters of conflict that affect the whole church, beginning with disagreements over the place of Biblical criticism in the life of the church in the 1860's and continuing with disagreements over how to respond to polygamists joining the church in the mid-twentieth century, then the ordination of women later in the century, and, most recently, whether to bless same-sex unions. In response to all this, provinces, during the later decades of the twentieth century, have recognized a role for certain "instruments of communion":

- *The Archbishop of Canterbury*: in his person and ministry across the Communion, the archbishop has often been described as *primus inter pares*—first among equals—in other words, one who while the convener of meetings of bishops such as the Lambeth Conference and Primates'

Meeting, sits alongside them as an equal, though with a pastoral concern to foster unity. Understood in this way, the new paradigm finds expression in this phrase.

- *The Lambeth Conference*: Again, while it is the Archbishop of Canterbury who invites the bishops of the Anglican Communion to attend the conference, when they are together it is not in order to be instructed and directed by him but to join him in prayer, study, and discernment. Hence, this is a conference rather than a decision-making synod. In recent decades, this has been at Canterbury Cathedral and the campus of the University of Kent. Around 650 bishops were welcomed to the most recent Lambeth Conference in July 2022.

- *The Anglican Consultative Council*: In 1968, the bishops of the Lambeth Conference requested the establishment of a body representative of all sections of the churches (bishops, clergy, and laity) to coordinate international Anglican ecumenical and mission work. The anchoring of this in the new paradigm is shown in the way that the legislative bodies of all the provinces had to give their consent before the Anglican Consultative Council (ACC) first met in 1971. It has met regularly since. By including laity and clergy as well as bishops from each member church, it has become the most representative of the instruments and ensures that the laity have a voice in the work of the instruments. The eighteenth meeting of the ACC took place in Ghana in 2023 and the nineteenth will take place in Ireland in 2026.

- *The Primates' Meeting*: Since 1979, the Archbishop of Canterbury has invited the primates (i.e. the presiding bishop, senior archbishop or moderator) of the provinces of the Anglican Communion (currently 42) to join him for "leisurely thought, prayer, and deep consultation" (see further ACC 2016).

These bodies have been likened to musical instruments, each having its own distinctive voice, but their role is to work with each other to contribute to the harmony of the whole. Furthermore, "in recent years Anglicans have interpreted this movement outwards in terms of the Five Marks of Mission (see below). The Instruments of Communion are intended to serve these marks. The Marks of Mission are the proper horizon towards which the Instruments are directed" (ACC 2016).

In the recent past, as mentioned, the issues of women's ordination, human sexuality, and women in the episcopacy have been contentious across the Communion. When, in 1944, Florence Li Tim-Oi from Hong Kong became the first woman to be ordained as a priest, her own province saw the move as irregular and a controversial innovation (see Carpenter 1991,134–138). The Diocese of Hong Kong eventually authorized ordination of women in 1971, and this was soon followed by the Episcopal Church ordaining women of its own in the United States in 1974, although this was regularized only in 1976 following authorization by the General Convention. By the beginning of the third millennium, another ten or so provinces had authorized the ordination of women. Those who were opposed saw the practice as contrary to Anglican biblical teaching and ecclesiology as well as lacking in cultural and pastoral sensibilities. The general trend around the Communion, however, shows that women's ordination is increasingly gaining ground in every continent and many Anglo-Catholics and Evangelicals who initially opposed it are now supportive of it.

The 1978 Lambeth Conference discussed the matter and passed a resolution, which affords an important insight into Anglican ecclesiology. The Conference recognized, "the autonomy of each of [the Communion's] member Churches, acknowledging the legal right of each Church to make its own decision about the appropriateness of admitting [. . .] women to Holy Orders." The Conference also observed that unilateral action "has consequences of the utmost significance for the Anglican Communion as a whole" and affirmed the Communion's "commitment to the preservation of unity within and between all member Churches of the Anglican Communion" (Anglican Communion 1978: Resolution 21, para. 3). These decisions show that ecclesial authority is vested within the member church and, as such, matters can only be properly resolved at that level, though sensitivity to the views of other member churches is also needed. Once again, the new paradigm is seen to be calling the shots.

But some issues have challenged this. On the question of consecrating women into the episcopate, the 1978 Lambeth Conference recommended "that no decision to consecrate be taken without consultation with the episcopate through the Primates and overwhelming support in any member church and in the diocese concerned, lest the bishop's office should become a cause for disunity instead of a focus of unity" (Resolution 22,

1978). The reference to "through the Primates" hints at the importance of interdependence and the desire to seek the mind of the whole church. But it is also clear that theological, doctrinal, or pastoral reasons for *or* against women's episcopacy are left to the local church to determine as long as episcopal authority guides such decisions. Since then, around half of the provinces have taken this step, though in many cases there has been opposition from some quarters within each province. The search for consensus has not succeeded in so far as some of these churches are left with a minority who cannot accept the episcopal orders of women or of those who have consecrated them. This has resulted in churches creating awkward structures in which both points of view stand alongside each other in tension, though usually with mutual respect.

The same cannot be said for the issue of whether to bless those in same-sex unions. In 2002, the Diocese of New Westminster, in the Anglican Church of Canada, unilaterally authorized a liturgy for the blessing of same-sex unions. This was an innovation with potentially serious consequences for the unity of the church, not least because liturgy is usually seen as a vessel of doctrinal expression within Anglicanism. A year later, the diocese of New Hampshire in The Episcopal Church elected and consecrated Gene Robinson, a priest in an active same-sex union. These developments caused further divisions. In the 2008, over 300 bishops, mainly from Global South provinces, declined to attend the Lambeth Conference. A number of evangelically aligned Episcopalian parishes have since broken away from The Episcopal Church, forming the Anglican Church in North America (ACNA). The Lambeth

Conference of 2018 was postponed to avoid a repeat of the divisions of 2008. The divisions continue at various levels, most recently revived over proposals from the Church of England's General Synod to authorize prayers for those in same-sex civil partnerships.

In 2008, around 300 active and retired bishops and 1200 others attended the Global Anglican Future Conference (GAFCON) in Jerusalem. It issued a "Jerusalem Declaration," a fourteen-point statement which explained its theological stance (GAFCON 2008). The statement presented a view of Anglican ecclesiology and ecclesial identity based on the historic formularies understood as propositions of "orthodox doctrine." Article 4 of the Jerusalem Declaration, for example, "upholds the Thirty-nine Articles as containing the true doctrine of the church." Article 7 upheld the Anglican ordinal and affirmed the three-fold ministry "in historic succession." Articles 11 and 13 were particularly emphatic that unity must be subservient to "orthodoxy." It was noteworthy that the drafters singled out for recognition only "those Anglicans who uphold orthodox faith and practice" (Article 11). Further, Article 13 stated, "We reject the authority of those churches and leaders who have denied the orthodox faith in word or deed." This embodied the view that episcopal authority is derivative and that primary fidelity should be to the scriptures and historic formularies, understood in a particular propositional way, a way which other Anglicans also claiming orthodoxy would not recognize. All of this demonstrated that the new paradigm of Anglican provinces being in a fraternity of equals in which authority comes from the finding of consensus was not accepted by those who supported this declaration. Instead, it is clear that for them authority is still understood in a hierarchical way, albeit one that replaced the British monarch with a set of magisterial propositions.

A different ecclesiological development has been a growing consensus around a definition of mission in the life of the church. This has been through the development and adoption of "The Five Marks of Mission." originating around the edges of the Anglican Consultative Council and now widely affirmed across churches of the Anglican Communion (Zink 2017). As the Anglican Communion website states, "The Five Marks of Mission are an important statement on mission. They express the Anglican Communion's common commitment to, and understanding of, God's holistic and integral mission [...]"

The mission of the Church is the mission of Christ:

1. To proclaim the Good News of the Kingdom
2. To teach, baptize and nurture new believers
3. To respond to human need by loving service
4. To transform unjust structures of society, to challenge violence of every kind and pursue peace and reconciliation
5. To strive to safeguard the integrity of creation, and sustain and renew the life of the earth (Anglican Communion 2020).

Important clarification of the definition occurred through the *MISSIO* report of 2000. It showed that the first mark of mission, identified at ACC-6 in 1984 with personal evangelism, is now recognized as "a summary of what *all* mission is about, because it is based on Jesus' own summary of his mission" (Matthew 4:17; Mark 1:14–15; Luke 4:18; Luke 7:22; cf. John 3:14–17). "Instead of being just one (albeit the first) of five distinct activities, this should be the key statement about *everything* we do in mission" (*MISSIO* 2000,19, italics original).

This insight adjusted the meaning of the Five Marks as a whole. They were no longer being seen as descriptions of different church activities but as descriptions of the way God's people participate in the coming of Christ's kingdom. The christological foundation of the Marks, made clear by the introductory sentence, was now being now underlined with an indication of their eschatological goal. In other words, they are understood as marks of an integral mission that comes from God in Christ and leads to his eschatological kingdom, one in which Anglicans participate in a variety of ways. This includes environmental action as well as responding to the needs of individual people and societies.

This perspective also incorporated worship within mission, because worship also proclaims the gospel: "An important feature of Anglicanism is our belief that worship is central to our common life. But worship is not just something we do alongside our witness to the good news: worship is itself a witness to the world" (*MISSIO* 2000,19). The proclamation of the kingdom, which summaries all the Marks, therefore includes proclamation through worship as well as in other activities: "Each time we celebrate the eucharist, we proclaim Christ's death until he comes (1Cor.11.26). Our liturgical life is a vital dimension of our mission calling and although it is not [explicitly] included in the Five Marks, it undergirds the forms of public witness listed there (*MISSIO* 2000,19).

From 2010 onwards, the Five Marks of Mission became ubiquitous across the Anglican Communion and beyond (Zink 2017). It has become clear that they have given Anglicanism a practicable theological definition of mission that is used at many different levels and in different ways.

Since ACC-16, this focus on mission has found particular expression in a "Season of Intentional Discipleship," an initiative that was launched from the floor by delegates at ACC-16 in Lusaka in 2016. The Season will run until ACC-19 in 2026 and has become a growing movement across the whole communion "to encourage *every* Anglican and *every* Anglican Church to live, love and be like Jesus—in *every* part of life—for the sake of the whole creation and to the glory of God" (Anglican Communion 2016, italics original). This was re-affirmed at ACC-17 in 2019 and expresses a growing missiological unity in Anglican ecclesial life that counteracts divisions over human sexuality, one that has not been imposed from the top down but has come about through an emerging consensus. Here, then, at the end of our historical survey, is another example of the new paradigm of Anglican life taking root across the Anglican Communion. Future decades will reveal if this paradigm continues to grow and become embedded or whether alternative hierarchical paradigms reassert themselves in different regions of the world.

References

Anglican Consultative Council, *The Virginia Report*, www.anglican communion.org/media/150889/report-1.pdf.

Anglican Consultative Council, *Towards A Symphony of Instruments*, 2016, www.anglicancommunion.org/ media/209979/Towards-a -Symphony-of-Instruments-Web-Version.pdf.

Anglican Communion, *The Chicago-Lambeth Quadrilateral*, 1888, www.anglicancommunion.org/media/109011/Chicago-Lambeth -Quadrilateral.pdf.

Anglican Communion, "An Appeal to All Christian People," Resolution 9 of the Lambeth Conference of 1920, https://www .anglicancommunion.org/media/127731/1920.pdf.

Anglican Communion, *Lambeth Conference 1930 resolutions*, https://www.anglicancommunion.org/media/127734/1930 .pdf?year=1930.

Anglican Communion, *Lambeth Conference 1978 resolutions*, www .anglicancommunion.org/media/127746/1978.pdf.

Anglican Communion, *The Anglican Communion Covenant*, 2009, www.anglicancommunion.org/media/99905/The_Anglican _Covenant.pdf.

Anglican Communion, *Ecumenical Dialogues*, 2019, www.anglican communion.org/ecumenism/ecumenical-dialogues.aspx.

Anglican Communion, 2020, www.anglicancommunion.org/mission /marks-of-mission.aspx.

Anglican Communion, 2016, www.anglicancommunion.org/mission /intentional-discipleship.aspx.

Anglican and Roman Catholic International Commission, *The Final Report*, 1981, www.christianunity.va/content/unitacristiani/en /dialoghi/sezione-occidentale/comunione-anglicana/dialogo /arcic-i/testo-in-inglese.html.

Anglican and Roman Catholic International Commission II, *Church as Communion*, (1990) www.anglicancommunion.org /media/105242/ARCIC_II_The_Church_as_Communion.pdf.

Avis, P. and Guyer, B. M., *The Lambeth Conference: Theology, History, Polity, and Purpose* (London: T and T Clark, 2017).

David Paton, R.O.: *The Life and Times of Bishop Hall of Hong Kong* (Diocese of Hong Kong and Macau, 1985).

Carpenter, Edward, *Archbishop Fisher, His Life and Times* (London: Canterbury Press, 1991).

Chapman, Mark 2020, "Early steps on the path to unity" (*The Church Times* 14th August 2020).

Church of England, The, *The Book of Common Prayer, including the Article of Religion and the Ordinal* (Cambridge: Cambridge University Press, 2004).

GAFCON, *The Jerusalem Declaration of 2008*, https://www.gafcon .org/jerusalem-2018/.

GAFCON, *Report on GAFCON's Bishops Training Institute Inaugural Conference*, 2016, https://www.gafcon.org/resources/.

IARCCUM (International Anglican Roman Catholic Commission for Unity and Mission), *Common Declaration of Pope John Paul II and the Archbishop of Canterbury Dr Robert Runcie*, 2016, https:// iarccum.org/archive/1982_common_declaration.pdf

Jacob, W. M, *The Making of the Anglican Communion Worldwide* (London: SPCK, 1997).

Jerusalem Declaration, 2008, https://www.gafcon.org/jerusalem -2018/.

MISSIO, 2000 (Mission Commission of the Anglican Communion— *MISSIO*), *Anglicans in Mission: A Transforming Journey: Report to the Anglican Consultative Council meeting in Edinburgh 1999* (London: SPCK), www.anglicancommunion.org/media/108016

/MISSIO-The-Standing-Commission-for-Mission-of-the
-Anglican-Communion.pdf.

Radner, Ephraim, "Christian Mission and the Lambeth Conferences," in Paul Avis and Benjamin M. Guyer (eds), *The Lambeth Conference: Theology, History, Polity and Purpose*, London: T&T Clark, 2017).

Ross, Alexander, *A still more excellent way: Authority and polity in the Anglican Communion* (London: SCM Press, 2020).

Windsor Report, *The Lambeth Commission on Communion*, Anglican Communion Office, 2004, www.anglicancommunion.org/media/68225/windsor2004full.pdf.

Ward, Kevin, *A History of Global Anglicanism* (Cambridge: Cambridge University Press, 2006).

World Council of Churches, 1982, *Baptism, Eucharist and Ministry*, www.oikoumene.org/sites/default/files/Document/FO1982_111_en.pdf.

Zink, Jesse, "Five Marks of Mission: History, Theology, Critique," *Journal of Anglican Studies*, Vol. 15.2 (Cambridge: Cambridge University Press, 2017.

CHAPTER THREE

Towards the Renewal of Anglican Identity as Communion[1]

Simon Ro Chul Lai,
Dean of Graduate School of Theology
at Sungkonghoe (Anglican) University.

This chapter is inspired and motivated by a growing awareness of a need for the transformation of static and tribal thinking and polity in the life of the Anglican Communion— what I have called the notion of "Anglican tribal identity." I hope to show that static thinking creates a static theological climate in the life of the church, thereby predefining and polarising issues, in particular the issue of homosexuality. This has created a barrier between churches and individuals in the Anglican Communion.

A static way of thinking is the principal cause and nature of the current crisis over the divisions of the Anglican Communion, disconnecting the activity of its life from the life of "the triune God's dynamic relationships," which implies the intrinsic "mutual indwelling" and "self-giving and receiving" which exist in the life of the Trinity. Mutual indwelling allows the three divine persons to share in one another's life, through a process

---

1. I have used part of my Ph.D. thesis for this paper. Ro, Chul-Lai, "Towards the Renewal of Anglican Identity as Communion: The Relationship of the Trinity, *Missio Dei*, and Anglican Comprehensiveness" (Ph.D. thesis, Cardiff University, 2009).

of reciprocal "permeability," and thus creates unity in diversity without any dissolution or any inequality. So, I write this chapter in order to suggest a dynamic and relational thinking about the Anglican Communion—what I have called the notion of "Anglican identity as Communion," which I hope transcends boundaries created by static thinking and thus can prepare the way for renewed dialogue for reconciliation which would release the current deadlock.

Is the Anglican experiment over?

On October 20, 2009, the Pontifical Council for the Doctrine of the Faith issued a papal decree on the Apostolic Constitution *Anglicanorum coetibus* which eases the requirements for transferring from the Anglican Church to the Catholic Church. Cardinal William Levada, Perfect of the Congregation for the Doctrine of the Faith, announced that the decree is "a new provision responding to the many requests that have been submitted to the Holy See from groups of Anglican clergy and faithful in different parts of the world who wish to enter into full visible communion with the Catholic Church."[2]

It is beyond the scope of this chapter, as well as the limits of space, to go into the specifics of why certain groups of believers

2. APOSTOLIC CONSTITUTION ANGLICANORUM COETIBUS PROVIDING FOR PERSONAL ORDINARIATES FOR ANGLICANS ENTERING INTO FULL COMMUNION WITH THE CATHOLIC CHURCH, 09.11.2009 <https://press.vatican.va/content/salastampa/it/bollettino/pubblico/2009/11/09/0696/01642.html [accessed March 2024].

and clergy in the Anglican Church made these requests to the Holy See. Just to keep this post on topic, I briefly mention here a challenging comment made by one of the clergy who converted to the Catholic Church through this papal decree, Monsignor John Broadhurst, a former bishop of the Church of England and now a priest of the Catholic Church in England, before he left the Church of England. To summarize his remarks:

> Anglicanism has become a joke because it has singularly failed to deal with any of its contentious issues [in particular, the issues of women bishops and homosexuality]. There is widespread dissent across the Communion. We are divided in major ways on major issues and the Communion has unraveled. I believed in the Church I joined, but it has been revealed to have no doctrine of its own. I personally think it has gone past the point of no return. The Anglican experiment is over.[3]

What is the Anglican experiment about, that the Monsignor invalidates? To add my own remarks to Monsignor's, albeit a bit roughly, it is the experiment of "unity in diversity," which is the corrective for how to see Anglicanism. In other words, the experiment in the acceptance of mutual differences among the principles that are alive in the Anglican Communion—the Catholic, Evangelical, and Broad/liberal elements based on reason and experience—is no longer possible within the Church

---

3. Church of England bishop says "Anglican experiment is over' https://www.catholicnewsagency.com/news/17493/church-of-england-bishop-says-anglican-experiment-is-over [accessed March 2024].

of England. The result is a lack of a proper concept of "authority" within the Church of England, which has led to a failure to deal adequately with the recent controversial issues of homosexuality and women bishops.

Is Broadhurst right about the demise of the Anglican experiment? The Anglican conviction and pride in the experiment in unity in diversity can only be achieved through a process of mutual acceptance of difference. This happens through a process of deconstruction and reconstruction through ongoing study, dialogue, and debate. As is assumed in this book series on Anglican conversations, such relationality cannot happen through an empty rhetorical flourish. Should we sit back and watch as a second or third Monsignor Broadhurst emerges? What should we do in the face of such division and conflict in our community?

This chapter is one theological response to these challenging questions that are being asked both within and outside of the Anglican Communion. More specifically, how can diverse and sometimes contradictory claims to truth coexist within the one and same Anglican Communion? The purpose of this chapter is, therefore, to develop a new way of thinking about Anglican identity as Communion, one which could transcend the boundaries created by static thinking and thus provide another way forward through the current deadlock. In order to fulfil this purpose, I first examine the underlying causes that are currently driving the Anglican Communion to the crisis of extreme division.

The Anglican Communion in crisis

The current crisis

Those Churches prepared to take on the notion of an Anglican Covenant as an expression of their responsibility to each other were also willing to limit their local freedoms for the sake of a wider church witness.[4] Some churches, however, were not willing to do this. They arrived at a situation where there were constituent Churches in covenant in the Anglican Communion and other churches in association, still bound by historic and perhaps personal links. Those Churches in covenant and those in association fed from many of the same sources, but not bound in a single and unrestricted sacramental communion, and certainly not sharing the same constitutional structures.[5]

These churches of communion or association were the focus of the former Archbishop of Canterbury, Dr. Rowan Williams'

---

4. The Windsor Report was published in late 2004 to address the nature of communion following "the decisions of The Episcopal Church (TEC) to appoint a priest in a committed same sex relationship as one of its bishops, and of the Diocese of New Westminster to authorize services for use in connection with same sex unions." *The Windsor Report 2004 of the Lambeth Commission on Communion* (Harrisburg, Pennsylvania: Morehouse Publishing, 2004), 4, hereafter referred to as *The Windsor Report*. In the Report (paragraphs 113–120, see Appendix Two: Proposal for the Anglican Covenant), an Anglican Covenant was proposed to provide a structural solution to divisions and conflicts related to the issue of homosexuality within the Anglican Communion.

5. Rowan Williams, "The Challenge and Hope of Being an Anglican Today: A Reflection for the Bishops, Clergy and Faithful of the Anglican Communion" *Anglican Communion News Service (ACNS)*, no. 4161 (2006) <http://www. anglicancommunion.org/acns/aricles/41/50/acns4161.cfm> [accessed July 2006].

statement, *The Challenge and Hope of Being an Anglican Today: A Reflection for the Bishops, Clergy and Faithful of the Anglican Communion,* following the 2006 TEC (The Episcopal Church) General Convention's incomplete response to the Windsor Report.[6] This would seem to indicate that a formal split within the Anglican Communion may be necessary. Conflicting views on homosexuality, the consecration of women to the episcopate, the loss of confidence in the Church's leadership, and the loss of confidence in its unity in diversity (a hallmark of Anglicanism)[7] exacerbated greatly the divisions of the Anglican Communion.

The nature of the crisis: what kind of Anglican identity?

On the surface, it appears as if the current crisis over the divisions of the Anglican Communion stems from conflicting views on homosexuality due to differing interpretations of Scripture between "traditionalists" and "liberals" within the Anglican Communion. Here it is possible to understand the current

---

6. The 75th TEC General Convention in 2006 has failed to meet the demands of the Windsor Report. The General Convention adopted a dilute resolution of a moratorium on the consecrations of practicing homosexual bishops.

7. The term "Anglicanism" signifies the faith, doctrine, and practice of the churches of the Anglican Communion, which is "historically descended from the Church of England." Borden W. Painter, "Bishop Walter H. Gray and the Anglican Congress of 1954," *Historical Magazine of the Protestant Episcopal Church* xlix: 2 (June 1980), 158, cited in J. Robert Wright, "Anglicanism, *Ecclesia Anglicana,* and Anglican: An Essay on Terminology," in Stephen Sykes, John Booty, and Jonathan Knight (eds.), *The Study of Anglicanism,* 477.

debates on the divisions of the Communion as one of selective polemics.

In September 2006, Anglican Primates met in Kigali.[8] The so-called Global South Primates rejected homosexual practices as incompatible with Scripture and saw it as a symptom of a decaying secular society. They supported Archbishop Williams' development of the Windsor Report's proposal for an Anglican Covenant, stating their belief that it "will demonstrate to the world that it is possible to be a truly global communion where differences are not affirmed at the expense of faith and truth but within the framework of a common confession of faith and mutual accountability."[9] The Kigali Communiqué called for a "separate ecclesiastical structure of the Anglican Communion in the USA," declaring the fact that the decisions of the 2006 TEC, General Convention raise "profound questions on the nature of Anglican identity across the entire Communion."[10]

---

8. The primates from the Global South gathered in Kigali, Rwanda in September 2006 in order to discuss a separate structure in the USA pertaining to the issue of homosexuality. See "The 2006 Kigali Communiqué" (2006) <http:// www.globalsouthanglican.org/index.php/comments/kigali_communique/> [accessed December 2006]. Hereafter referred to as "The 2006 Kigali Communiqué."

9. "The 2006 Kigali Communiqué." There are two polarising views on homosexuality within the Anglican Communion today. One view represented by the Anglican churches in the Global South which rejects homosexual practice as incompatible with Scripture and as the advocacy of decaying secular society. The other represented by North America, which supports homosexuality as "a faith-filled development in the ongoing life of the Anglican Communion." Ian T. Douglas, "Anglicans Gathering for God's Mission: A Missiological Ecclesiology for the Anglican Communion," *Journal of Anglican Studies*, vol. 2.2 (December 2004), 12. Hereafter referred to as "Anglicans Gathering for God's Mission."

10. "The 2006 Kigali Communiqué."

It is, however, very significant to realize that the current divisions of the Anglican Communion fundamentally relate to the fragmentation of its collective life as such (its unity, authority, and identity) rather than to disagreement on a particular issue such as homosexuality or women bishops. In other words, the issue of division of the Church is not simply a single matter of theological polemics but a matter complicated by the political, economic, and cultural realities of the Church's life.

The rapidly changing demography of the Anglican Communion and globalization espoused by one multinational economic system (capitalism) and the single "mega-power" of the United States affect the debates over unity, authority, and identity in the contemporary Anglican Communion.[11] Resulting from the crisis of the Western church-centered mission strategies in the post-World War II era. Following the end of colonialism, the question of identity has been exacerbated within the Anglican Communion and in particular in sister and brother churches from the Global South.[12] At present, the Anglican churches in the Global South consider themselves to be the predominant church within the Anglican Communion, claiming that they

---

11. See Ian T. Douglas, "Anglicans Gathering for God's Mission," 10–11.

12. According to David Barrett, Anglican mission scholar, 83% of the 522 million Christians in the world lived in Europe or North America in the year 1900. In the year 1996, only 41% of Christians in the world lived in the same area. Barrette predicts that in the 2025, 70% of the world's Christians will live in Africa, Asia, Latin America, and the Pacific. See David B. Barret, "Annual Statistical Table on Global Mission: 1996," *International Bulletin of Missionary Research* 20 (January 1996), 24–25, cited in Ian T. Douglas, "Anglican identity and the *Missio Dei*: Implications for the American Convocation of Churches in Europe," *Anglican Theological Review*, vol. 82, no. 3 (2000), 461.

have more than 70 per cent of the active membership of the worldwide Anglican Communion.[13] In contrast, the political, economic, cultural, and military dominance of the United States has caused TEC to see itself as the pre-eminent church in the Anglican Communion.[14]

All these sectarian and superior impulses have resulted in ambiguities in the balance of relationship between power, unity, and the sources of authority within the Anglican Communion and have thus caused it to be faced with the crisis of division. I, therefore, argue that what really is behind the current conflict over homosexuality is missiological and ecclesiological—what I call *missio-ecclesiological* conflicts over unity and authority, which implies the conflict over the subject of Anglican identity as it affects Anglican approaches to the relationship between unity and authority.[15]

The question of the identity of the Anglican Communion (Anglican identity) has appeared on the official agenda of all sorts of conferences within the worldwide Anglican Communion whenever it has confronted the crisis brought by disagreement on a specific issue. The answer to this question has been made through asking the Anglican Communion itself the following interconnected questions: 1) What is the purpose and nature of

---

13. See "The 2006 Kigali Communiqué."

14. See Ian T. Douglas, "Anglicans Gathering for God's Mission," 11.

15. I use the term "missio-ecclesiological" with a view to emphasising that both the Church and mission are inseparable. The faith of the Church is intrinsically missionary. As David Bosch says: "Christianity is missionary by its very nature or it denies its very *raison d'être*." David J. Bosch, *Transforming Mission: Paradigm Shifts in Theology of Mission* (Maryknoll, New York: Orbis Books, 1991), 9. Hereafter referred to as *Transforming Mission*.

the Church?; and, 2) How has it conveyed the purpose and nature of the Church within its own historical tradition? When these considerations are taken together, we are able to understand the two following things. Firstly, the question of Anglican identity is essentially *missio-ecclesiological*. This refers to what kind of mission the Church is called to be. Secondly, the question of Anglican identity is a matter of how the Anglican Communion has shared the Christian faith in terms of addressing differences in understanding. In this respect, the question of Anglican identity might be viewed as a matter of the relationship between unity and authority, which is a way of shaping the Communion into unity.

In order to discuss the issue of Anglican identity in this chapter, I shall, therefore, use the term identity as a way of expressing the relationship between unity and authority; that is, a way of expressing how authority is related to unity. I argue that at present there are two differing and conflicting perceptions of Anglican identity within the Anglican Communion as either "Communion" or "tribal identity," leading to two different Anglican approaches to the relationship between unity and authority. Before beginning further discussion on these two notions of Anglican identity, I shall examine Anglican self-understanding in the context of both unity and authority.

Anglican understanding of the nature of unity and authority

The 1997 Virginia Report and the 2004 Windsor Report give helpful insights into Anglican self-understanding in this respect.

They considered in some depth the meaning and nature of unity and authority in addressing the question of the unity of the Anglican Communion following the proposal of the 1985 General Convention of TEC on the consecration of women to the episcopate and the election and consecration of Gene Robinson, who was living in a sexual relationship with a partner of the same sex in 2003.

The nature of Anglican unity

The Virginia Report describes Anglican unity as "a diversity held together in God's unity and love"[16]: "The unity of the Anglican Communion derives from the unity given in the triune God, whose inner personal and relational nature is communion."[17] The Virginia Report continues: "The eternal, mutual, self-giving and receiving love of the three persons of the Trinity is the source and ground of our communion, of our fellowship with God and one another."[18] This would indicate that the idea of Trinitarian communion is inherent to Anglican unity. This concept needs further discussion.

---

16. *The Virginia Report of the Inter-Anglican Theological and Doctrinal Commission* in *Being Anglican in the Third Millennium, Panama 1996,* in James M. Rosenthal and Nicola Currie (eds.), *The Official Report of the 10th Meeting of the Anglican Consultative Council X, Panama City* (Harrisburg, Pennsylvania: Morehouse Publishing, 1997), 237, para. 2.9. Hereafter referred to as *The Virginia Report.*

17. Ibid., 233, para. 1.11.

18. Ibid., 237, para 2.9.

Trinitarian communion

The general understanding of Christians about God's being and acts is expressed in terms of the Trinity. We cannot recognize God's being without "the mediating role of the Son and inspiration of the Spirit"[19]; the experience of God is "not of three personal realities in isolation from each other, but of persons in relations, always interweaving and interpenetrating each other."[20] This implies that God has to be understood relationally and communally: "Father, Son and Holy Spirit, who mutually indwell one another, exist in one another and for one another, in interdependent giving and receiving."[21] It is the life of Trinitarian communion—what I call *the life of the triune God's dynamic relationships*.

This life of the triune God's dynamic relationships, which implies the intrinsic "mutual indwelling" and "self-giving and receiving" which exist in the life of the Trinity, allows the three divine persons to share in one another's life, through a process of reciprocal "permeability,"[22] and thus create unity in diversity

---

19. Robin Greenwood, *Transforming Priesthood: A New Theology of Mission and Ministry* (London: SPCK, 1994), 78. Hereafter referred to as *Transforming Priesthood*.

20. Paul S. Fiddes, *Participating in God: A Pastoral Doctrine of the Trinity* (London: Darton, Longman and Todd, 2000), 6. Hereafter referred to as *Participating in God*.

21. *Eucharistic Presidency* (London: Church House Publishing, 1997), 2.6., cited in *Mission-Shaped Church: Church Planting and Fresh Expressions of Church in a Changing Context* (London: Church House Publishing, 2004), 84–85. Hereafter referred to as *Mission-Shaped Church*.

22. I owe my use of the word "permeability" to Lorraine Cavanagh who uses it in the following terms: "The *Via Media* continues to be seen as the hallmark of Anglican identity and this is a helpful interpretation of the spirit of Anglicanism.

without any dissolution or any inequality. The dynamic and relational life of Trinitarian communion is at the heart of the understanding of the Trinity.

Anglican unity in trinitarian communion

The Windsor Report describes Anglican unity in Trinitarian communion in the following words: "We are, by God's gift, in communion with the Persons of the Holy Trinity, and are members of one another in Christ Jesus. We are, in the power of the Spirit, sent into all the world to declare that Jesus is Lord. This grace-given and grace-full mission from God, and communion with God, determine our relationship with one another."[23] Accordingly, the importance of intrinsic "relatedness" and "communion" in the life of the Trinity applies to our understanding of the nature of Anglican unity. It indicates that Anglican unity must be characterized primarily by both relatedness and communion, not by an instrumental or formal structure. In other words, whatever

---

If we understand the 'middle way' as signifying neither inconclusive compromise, or an unstructured synthesis of 'inclusive' theologies, but a dynamic holding together of difference in the ongoing life of the Spirit of Jesus Christ, we begin to see how the concept of locality might help to free Anglicans into a more dynamic unity. It could provide Anglicans with a conceptual 'middle' space in which to forge new friendships across old divisions. It now becomes especially important to retain a sense of the innate 'permeability' of Anglicanism. When brought together, the two concepts of permeability and dynamic allow for the possibility of movement to take place across existing boundaries in the life of communion." Lorraine Cavanagh, "The Freeing of Anglican Identities," *Theology Wales* (2004), 22.

   23. *The Windsor Report*, 12, para. 5.

the presenting issues, the imposition of an exclusive structural and instrumental approach to the maintenance of the ongoing life of the Anglican Communion may prevent the creation of Anglican unity. As Carlos Calvani points out: "'Communion'" is not sustained by the consensus of ideas but by the disposition to accept others with their differences, just as Christ embraces and accepts us."[24]

I have briefly outlined an Anglican understanding of unity as one which is patterned on that of Trinitarian communion. I have illustrated this by drawing on the intrinsic relatedness and communion which exist in the life of the Trinity. The need emerges for an Anglican understanding of the nature of authority in considering the following question: How is this kind of unity in Trinitarian communion to be achieved in the ongoing life of the Anglican Communion?

The nature of Anglican authority

The 1948 Lambeth Conference identified the nature of Anglican authority as a "dispersed authority." According to the statement of the Conference, this dispersed authority, which derives from the relational and communal nature of the divine Trinity, is "a process of mutual support and mutual checking,"[25] which

---

24. Carlos Calvani, "The Myth of [the] Anglican Communion," *Journal of Anglican Studies*, vol. 3.2 (December 2005), 151.

25. "The Meaning and Unity of the Anglican Communion" from a Committee of Bishops reporting on "The Anglican Communion," in The Lambeth Conference 1948: The Encyclical Letter from the Bishops; together with Resolutions and Reports (London: SPCK, 1948), Part II, 95. Hereafter referred to as The 1948 Lambeth Conference.

binds the Anglican Communion together. This indicates that Anglican authority should be understood not as a static norm but as one of dynamic and relational means for being unified in the triune God. In other words, Anglican authority is not a centralized power or static system for expressing and shaping unity. Rather, it is one of God's instruments for embodying the unity given in the triune God, participating in His mission for the world.

The 2004 Windsor Report embodies this kind of dynamic and relational nature of dispersed Anglican authority in describing the relationship between the authority of the triune God and that of Scripture. According to the Windsor Report, the authority of Scripture is one of the diverse vehicles of the triune God's authority for His purpose for the world.

At the same time, the diverse and relational nature of dispersed Anglican authority has raised the following key question: How much diversity is to be allowed in today's, to some extent, fragmented and individualistic Anglican Communion due to the different parties (catholic, evangelical, and liberal) within it? Notwithstanding the fact that the nature of Anglicanism is rooted in an ethos in which a constant dynamic interplay of Scripture, tradition, and reason is the characteristic way to Anglican unity,[26] each party clings to its own sources of authority—catholic to the Church's traditional order, in particular episcopacy, evangelical to Scripture, and liberal to its

---

26. The Anglican understanding of the relationship between Scripture, tradition, and reason was well summarized in the Virginia Report. See *The Virginia Report*, 244–245, paras. 3.5–3.11.

belief in reason or experience.[27] As a result, they are still in a conflicting tension.

Two principles of dispersed Anglican authority: "adiaphora" and "subsidiarity"

Traditionally, the provincial autonomy within the Anglican Communion has been framed by the two following core principles of dispersed Anglican authority: "Adiaphora" and "Subsidiarity." The principle of "Adiaphora," which signifies literally "things that do not make a difference,"[28] has been formulated to express a key distinction between core doctrines of the Anglican Communion, namely between essentials and non-essentials. The principle of "Subsidiarity," which implies "the principle that matters should be decided as close to the local level as possible,"[29] has been formulated to express the importance of locality in Anglicanism as Jesus Christ became a human being within one particular culture, thereby resisting the temptation of centralism of the Anglican Communion.

---

27. Traditionally, there are three parties within the Anglican Communion: 1) The Catholic, strengthened and reshaped from 1830s by the Oxford Movement, which has emphasized the catholic tradition and ecclesiastical authority; 2) The Evangelical which has emphasized the importance of the Protestant aspects of the Church of England, stressing the centrality of the authority of Scripture as definitive for the Church; and, 3) The Liberal which has emphasized the significance of the use of reason or experience in theological exploration, stressing the need to develop Christian belief and practice in order to respond creatively to wider advances in human knowledge and understanding and the importance of social and political action in forwarding the kingdom of God.

28. *The Windsor Report*, 21, para. 36.

29. Ibid., 21, para. 38.

In short, the two core principles of autonomy with respect to the dispersed Anglican authority have been formulated to hold together across differences within the Anglican Communion. This indicates that autonomy of a dispersed Anglican authority should be understood not as unlimited freedom but "freedom-in-relation" or "autonomy-in-relation,"[30] as embracing differences. In other words, the autonomy of Anglican authority is "a form of limited authority"[31] on the basis of mutual responsibility and interdependence, not independence. In practice, the 1963 Anglican Congress, which considered in some depth the relationship between Anglican identity and *Missio Dei*, identified Anglican life in unity as directly connected with authority and communion, as "Mutual Responsibility and Interdependence in the Body of Christ."[32]

Consequently, the two characteristics of mutual responsibility and interdependence of Anglican autonomy, which are at the heart of the two core principles of "Adiaphora" and "Subsidiarity," have enabled the Anglican Communion to retain the spirit of dispersed Anglican authority within today's, to some extent, fragmented and individualistic Anglican Communion.

In my brief explanation of Anglican unity and authority, I have described the dynamic, relational, and communal nature of the triune God. In other words, the life of the triune God's dynamic relationships, which implies the intrinsic "mutual indwelling" and

---

30. Ibid., 35–36, paras. 76 and 80.

31. Ibid., 35, para. 77.

32. Since the first Congress was held in London in 1908, two more Congresses were held in Minneapolis in 1954 and in Toronto in 1963.

"self-giving and receiving" which exist in the life of the Trinity, is the source and ground of Anglican unity and authority.

This allows us to answer the previous question of how are the two notions of Anglican identity as either Communion or tribal identity to be described. Before answering this, in order to avoid confusion between the two terms, I shall examine a little more historical and etymological background to the way in which Anglican identity can be seen as either Communion or tribal identity.

Two notions of Anglican identity

As already stated, the question of Anglican identity is a missio-ecclesiological matter: What kind of Church, (the Anglican Communion as a body of people who belong to one another in God), is it called to become in mission? It, therefore, requires an exploration of the Anglican understanding of the purpose and nature of the Church, which could supply the principal source for understanding Anglican identity.

Anglican understanding of the purpose and nature of the Church

The foregoing discussion suggests that the dynamic and relational life of the triune God is a key to an understanding of the Trinity. This implies the two following things: First, God as Creator has called human beings to participate in His life of dynamic relationships and thus live in communion with one another, with the world, and with Himself.[33] It is the mission of God (*Missio Dei*) that is "to bring into being, sustain and perfect the whole creation," and that is "to restore and reconcile the fallen creation (Colossians 1.20)."[34]

Second, the Church is both "a sign and disclosure of the kingdom of God," and "the agent of his mission. It is the community, through whom he acts for the world's redemption," and it exists to bear witness to the life of the triune God's dynamic relationships.[35] In other words, the Church is an example and image of the life of the triune God's dynamic relationships. As Rowan Williams says: "[The Church is] the place where the life of the Holy Trinity is visibly active: the Spirit brings Christ alive in us, and that life is a life of adoration and self-giving directed towards God the Father."[36] In 1993 the Fifth World Conference on Faith and Order stated the purpose and nature of the Church as follows:

> It is in the Church that the Holy Spirit realizes this communion (koinonia). The Church is called to be, in the realm of spiritual life as well as in its commitment to the service of humanity and creation, in harmony with the plan of the Triune God revealed in the Scriptures. It is called, in the power of the Holy Spirit, to manifest

---

33. Also, see John 17.3. All biblical quotations in this paper are from The New Revised Standard Version of the Bible © 1989 unless otherwise stated.

34. *Mission-Shaped Church*, 85.

35. Ibid., 94 and 85. See Ephesians 3.10–11.

36. Rowan Williams, *Tokens of Trust: An Introduction to Christian belief* (London: Canterbury Press, 2007), 135. Hereafter referred to as *Tokens of Trust*.

the divine life holding out to the world the possibility of being enfolded within that divine life.[37]

What I have described therefore suggests that the Anglican Communion understands the purpose and nature of the Church as bearing witness to the very life of the triune God's dynamic relationships.

Dynamic thinking in the life of the Communion

This would indicate that the Anglican Communion regards itself as a communion which is in an ongoing state of relationship, participating in the life of the triune God's dynamic relationships—what I call *dynamic thinking*, rather than simply as "a federation or gathering which the words 'Church' or *ekklesia* sometimes signify." As John Zizioulas says:

> The Church is not simply an institution. She is a "mode of existence," *a way of being.* The mystery of the Church, even in its institutional dimension, is deeply bound to the being of man, to the being of the world and to the very being of God...It is a way of *relationship* with the world, with other people and with God, an event of *communion.*[38]

---

37. Thomas F. Best and Günter Gassmann (eds.), *On the Way to Fuller Koinonia* (Geneva: WCC Publications, 1994), 274–275.

38. John D. Zizioulas, *Being as Communion: Studies in Personhood and the Church* (Crestwood, New York: St Vladimir's Seminary Press, 1985), 15. Hereafter referred to as *Being as Communion.*

I propose to call this kind of dynamic thinking about the Anglican Communion the notion of *Anglican identity as Communion*. In order to emphasize the importance of intrinsic "dynamic relationships" in the life of Anglican identity as Communion, I shall therefore use the term "communion" as a description of the way in which its members participate in the life of the triune God's dynamic relationships. The 1988 Lambeth Conference expressed the term *Koinonia* (by implication, communion) not only as a way of describing the relation that exists not only between the Churches of the Anglican Communion but between Christians of different Churches by virtue of their common baptism, illustrating that "the New Testament uses the term *Koinonia* to describe both our fellowship with God (1 John 1.3 and 2 Pet. 1.4) and our fellowship with each other (Acts 2.42, 1 Cor.10.16, 17, 1 John 1.3)."[39]

When Anglican identity is understood as a communion, it indicates that the Anglican Communion does not claim to be normative for the Church. In other words, it does not regard itself as self-contained, complete, and autonomous and thus fundamentally disconnected from the life of other Churches or Christian groupings. Rather, the Anglican Communion believes that it is called to be a dynamic, relational, and transforming Church, one which reflects the life of the triune God's dynamic relationships. This thought is given expression in *Dogmatic*

---

39. *The Truth Shall Make You Free: The Lambeth Conference 1988* (London: The Anglican Consultative Council, 1988), 5. Hereafter referred to as *The Truth Shall Make You Free*. The 1988 Lambeth Conference put the issue of communion on the top of agenda for Anglicans, expecting the imminent election of a woman to the episcopate.

and Pastoral Concerns, one of the section reports of the 1988 Lambeth Conference:

The Anglican Communion consists of a family of Churches which say of themselves that they are in communion with each other. At a time when there is debate and disagreement in the family, it is essential to set all consideration of what it might mean to be Anglican in the wider context of the familiar and ancient (indeed biblical) word "communion." In the Collect for All Saints' Day widely used throughout the Anglican world, we hear of the whole Church in heaven and on earth being bound together in "one communion and fellowship."[40]

Static thinking in the life of the Communion

The recent currents in the Anglican Communion do not take account of this dynamic dimension of its life. The contemporary Anglican Communion's styles of life and behaviour have become separated from the life of the triune God's dynamic relationships. I call this development *static thinking*. The increased emphasis on "instruments of unity"[41] in the Anglican Communion is a clear example of this static phenomenon. The four instruments of unity have become "centralized decision-making bodies to dictate matters of identity and authority in

---

40. *The Truth Shall Make You Free*, p. 105, paras. 92–93.

41. There are the four instruments of unity as representing the polity of the Anglican Communion, which are the Anglican Consultative Council, the Lambeth Conference, the Primates' Meeting, and the Archbishop of Canterbury. The four instruments of unity are summarized in Section C: Our Future Life Together of the 2004 Windsor Report. See *The Windsor Report*, 41–46.

the Anglican Communion,"[42] notwithstanding the fact that the instruments of unity have said that they "do not favor the accumulation of formal power by the Instruments of Unity, or the establishment of any kind of central 'curia' for the Communion."[43]

Over the past fifty years, structural instruments of unity have become increasingly emphasized within the diversity of the Anglican Communion. "Two instruments of unity" in the Anglican Communion (the Archbishop of Canterbury and the Lambeth Conference) have now increased to "four instruments of unity" as the Anglican Consultative Council and the Primates Meeting were established in the 1970s. In particular, the Primates Meeting has increasingly been perceived as a "locus of authority for the global Communion,"[44] despite the fact that it has suggested that it has an "*enhanced responsibility* in offering guidance on doctrinal, moral and pastoral matters" rather than a "consultative and advisory authority."[45] The Primates Meeting occurs annually rather than every other year.

All this would indicate that a juridical and structural approach to maintaining the unity in diversity of the Anglican Communion may become increasingly dominant within the Communion. We see the dominance of the centralized "from above" authority in the Communion in the 2004 Windsor

---

42. Ian T. Douglas, "Anglicans Gathering for God's Mission," 18.

43. *The Windsor Report*, 44, para. 105.

44. Ian T. Douglas, "Anglicans Gathering for God's Mission," 8.

45. *The 2004 Windsor Report*, 44.

Report's emphasis on an exclusive structural/instrumental approach to the maintenance of the Communion with regard to the issue of homosexuality. As Harold Lewis says:

> Contract has replaced covenant as the way Anglican live, move, and have their being... [T]he Windsor Report runs the risk of becoming a Trojan horse, and that a precedent might be set for "centralized culturalization" of the Anglican Communion—in other words, it would become, in some ways, more like the Roman Catholic Church in its governance, thereby abandoning its historic Anglican ethos.[46]

As the foregoing discussions have revealed, the nature of Anglican unity and authority derives from the dynamic, relational, and communal nature of the triune God. That is to say that the life of the triune God's dynamic relationships, which implies the intrinsic "mutual indwelling" and "self-giving and receiving" which exist in the life of the Trinity is the source and ground of Anglican unity and authority. In this respect, whatever the presenting issues, the imposition of juridical and structural solutions to disagreements in the Anglican Communion today not only is incompatible with the nature of Anglican unity and authority but may also exacerbate the current divisions of the Communion.

I argue that this kind of juridical and structural response to the challenges of unity and authority constitutes a static situation in

---

46. Harold T. Lewis, "Covenant, Contract, and Communion: Reflections on a Post-Windsor Anglicanism," *Anglican Theological Reviews*, vol. 87, no. 4 (Fall 2005), 601 and 606.

the life of the Anglican Communion. We see this non-dynamic, or static, climate of thought increasingly dominating the life of the Communion at province, diocese, and parish level. Here we note the 2008 Global Anglican Future Conference (GAFCON) as an example of this static climate.

The 2008 Global Anglican Future Conference

GAFCON was held in Jerusalem from 22-29 June 2008. The conference, which was attended by 1,148 lay and clergy participants, including 291 Anglican bishops, was primarily aimed at "Anglican leaders who consider themselves to be in impaired communion with the global church because of the consecration in 2003 of openly homosexual bishop Gene Robinson by TEC."[47] The GAFCON statement claims that GAFCON has arisen because a false, or different, gospel which is contrary to the apostolic gospel is being promoted within the provinces of the Anglican Communion. According to the statement, a false gospel "undermines the authority of God's Word written and uniqueness of Jesus Christ as the author of salvation from sin, death and judgment," and thus promotes "a variety of sexual preferences and immoral behaviour as a universal human right."[48]

---

47. "Global Anglican Future Conference," *Wikipedia* <Global Fellowship of Confessing Anglicans - Wikipedia>. Also see the homepage of the GAFCON <https://www.gafcon.org/> [accessed March 2024].

48. "The GAFCON Final Statement," *The Global Anglican Future Conference*, Jerusalem, Israel, 2008.

Although GAFCON did not decide to create a formal schism in the Anglican Communion, it would implement immediate and prudent steps to prepare new ecclesiastical structures, particularly within the liberal provinces of North America:

> Our fellowship is not breaking away from the Anglican Communion. We, together with many other faithful Anglicans throughout the world, believe the doctrinal foundation of Anglicanism, which defines our core identity as Anglicans, is expressed in these words: The doctrine of the Church is grounded in the Holy Scripture and in such teachings of the ancient Fathers and Councils of the Church as are agreeable to the said Scriptures.[49]

Within Anglicanism, Scripture has always been recognized as the Church's supreme authority, and as such must be understood as a focus and means of the unity given in the triune God. In other words, the authority of Scripture is one of the diverse vehicles of the triune God's authority for his purpose for the world. Furthermore, as the foregoing discussion suggests, the Anglican Communion understands the purpose and nature of the Church as bearing witness to the very life of the triune God's dynamic relationships. In this respect, GAFCON's emphasis on "a false gospel" would seem to seek its own security and structure in the context of increasing

---

49. Ibid.

social and religious diversity. That is to say, GAFCON's static thinking and behaviour about Anglican identity creates a static theological climate and leads to static ways of defining Scripture and issues, creating a barrier between churches and individuals in the Anglican Communion.

Within the far wider Anglican Communion, we find that the same principle holds true with regard to the conflicts related to identity. Static thinking becomes self-referential and seeks its own security and structure, and thus disconnects the activity of the Communion from the life of the triune God's dynamic relationships. As a result of this, the Communion becomes a "tribal"[50] church which adheres to fixed beliefs which compete with each other for normative status, thus occupying static ways of defining Scripture and issues and subsequently God Himself. Peter Selby describes a tribal church as an "ethnic community," based on its own self-protection, which "is bound to start with the difficulties, with those who will be unable to accept change, with the pain that adjustment will cause to the existing community."[51] I propose to call this kind of static, tribal thinking about the Anglican Communion the notion of *Anglican tribal identity*, which contradicts the life of the triune God's dynamic relationships.

---

50. I owe my use of the word "tribal" to Peter Selby's idea of "a tribal church." See Peter Selby, *Belonging: Challenge to a Tribal Church* (London: SPCK, 1991). Hereafter referred to as *Belonging*.

51. Ibid., 44.

Anglican identity as Communion –
the relational approach

When Anglican identity is understood as a communion, it encourages the Anglican Communion to see the nature of the relationship between unity and authority as a relational and communal dynamic as it reflects the life of the triune God's dynamic relationships. In this case, authority is not a centralized power or system to maintain the Communion but a dynamic and participatory means to the unity given in the triune God. A dynamic understanding of the relationship between unity and authority therefore allows the Anglican Communion to hold to its inclusive attitude towards differences within the Communion and other denominations. It can be open to God's final purpose of embracing all creation in the world. In other words, this dynamic notion of Anglican identity as Communion enables the Communion to move away from a dominating and self-seeking perfection towards a responsible sharing in God's concern for the world.[52] This responsibility includes "caring for and confronting groups and institutions, inside and beyond the church, through evangelism, pastoral care, social and political concern, supporting the weak and opposing injustice and bringing help to those in need."[53]

---

52. Cf. Robin Greenwood, *Transforming Priesthood*, 65.

53. Ibid., 65.

Anglican tribal identity – the structural approach

In contrast, those who hold to a perspective of Anglican tribal identity are advocating structural and instrumental approaches to the maintenance of the Communion. They are preoccupied with static ways of defining the relationship between unity and authority. Their non-dynamic concept of Anglican identity has caused them to understand authority as a static and essential norm for the maintenance of the Communion rather than as part of a process of mutual support and mutual checking which binds the Communion together. As a result, for them, it appears as if authority has become an exclusive and sectarian means of expressing and shaping unity.

Anglicans who hold to this concept of tribal identity feel that taking seriously the realm of the notion of Communion puts their Christian identity at risk. This is because they are worried that the notion of Communion which has a relational and comprehensive nature may fall into a secularism which is incompatible with the Christian truth, as revealed in Scripture. As a result, they, as self-proclaimed true believers, hold exclusive and sectarian attitudes towards addressing differences in understanding. This is the notion of Anglican identity as tribal identity, which dominates the Anglican Communion today and which is found in the current debates on the divisions of the Communion pertaining to the issue of homosexuality.

Conflict between two notions of Anglican identity: the 2004 Windsor Report

The 2004 Windsor Report gives helpful insights into Anglican self-understanding in this respect. It considers in some depth the meaning and the nature of communion following the decisions of TEC to appoint a priest in a committed same-sex relationship as one of its bishops and of the Diocese of New Westminster in the Anglican church of Canada to authorize services for use in connection with same-sex unions.

In the Windsor Report, an Anglican Covenant (the Windsor Draft Covenant) was proposed to provide a structural solution to the current divisions and conflicts due to the different views on homosexuality. To end the current deadlock within the Anglican Communion, the Windsor Report was concerned to ask TEC to obey certain obligations. At the present time, the Windsor Report has caused Anglicans today to be confronted with a choice between the two opposing views on homosexuality.

Responding to the Windsor Report, Ian Douglas is concerned that a juridical and structural approach to the maintenance of the Anglican Communion has become increasingly dominant within the Communion:

> I am particularly thankful for: the authority it gives to Scripture, the biblical hermeneutics it advances, and the underlying emphasis on relationships as basic to a life in communion. I am concerned, however, with the [Windsor] report's overall emphasis on a structural

approach to the maintenance of communion. I am not convinced that a reification of the Instruments of Unity offers a life-giving approach to what it means to be an Anglican in today's world. I would much rather have seen a liturgical and missiological approach rather than a structural/instrumental trajectory.[54]

Vincent Strudwick also argues, presenting the meaning of Christian "covenant": "The covenant is not a set of doctrinal statements to which Churches sign up, but a relationship to which they are called. Thus, it is not a quick fix, but a way of enabling us to focus on our common mission."[55] In principle, the concept of Christian covenant rests on the relationship between God and His people, the Church. In other words, God made a covenant with His Church, calling it to be a witness to His steadfast love for the world.

When these considerations are taken together, we are able to describe Anglican understanding of the nature of covenant as expressing the life of the triune God's dynamic relationships. This suggests that the Anglican Communion does not regard covenant as a legal transaction and agreement for its own sake, which the term "contract" sometimes signifies.[56] Rather, the

---

54. Ian T. Douglas, "An American Reflects on the Windsor Report," *Journal of Anglican Studies*, vol. 3.2 (December 2005), 156.

55. Vincent Strudwick, "It's a relationship, not a doctrinal quiz," *Church Times* (7 July 2006), 8.

56. With regard to the idea of the relationship between covenant and contract, see Harold T. Lewis, "Covenant, Contract, and Communion: Reflections on a Post-Windsor Anglicanism," *Anglican Theological Review*, vol. 87, no. 4 (Fall 2005), 601–607.

Anglican Communion regards covenant as a way of being the Church, participating in the very life of the triune God's dynamic relationships. This indicates that the Windsor Draft Covenant's emphasis on a structural approach to the maintenance of the Communion should be reconsidered through a process of continuing conversation, reflecting the life of the triune God's dynamic relationships.

The present climate of the conflict in the Anglican Communion does not take account of this contemplative dimension of the nature of covenant. Since the Windsor Draft Covenant was proposed in 2004, the Anglican Covenant process has been established in order to consider the re-establishment of the life of communion in the Anglican Communion. Although three main stages (such as the Nassau Draft in 2007, the St. Andrew's Draft in 2008, and the Ridley-Cambridge Draft in 2009) have been developed,[57] they have significantly contributed to the legalization of the Covenant, undermining the nature of dispersed authority in the Communion in the future.

The most important thing is the fact that whatever the presenting issues, the imposition of an exclusive structural/instrumental approach to the maintenance of the ongoing life of the Anglican Communion is incompatible with both an Anglican understanding of the nature of covenant and

---

57. See the Anglican Communion official website on an Anglican Covenant for a more detailed understanding of the Anglican Covenant process, "An Anglican Covenant," <https://www.anglicancommunion.org/theology/doctrine/covenant.aspx 9> [accessed March 2024]. As the final version of the Anglican Covenant was completed, it is now with the Provinces of the Anglican Communion for formal consideration for adoption by each Province through appropriate processes.

authority. It is also not helpful in resolving the current crisis over the divisions of the Communion. In practice, the current structural/instrumental approaches (such as the Anglican Covenant process, the 2006 Kigali Communiqué, and the 2008 GAFCON) have failed to cope with the current crisis in the Communion. Rather, they have exacerbated the divisions of the Anglican Communion today.

Conclusion: the need for the renewal of Anglican identity as Communion

This raises the question of where this kind of exclusive and structural/instrumental approaches to the maintenance of the Anglican Communion comes from. In this chapter, I argued that static thinking about the Communion, which implies the concept of Anglican tribal identity, lies behind the current exclusive and structural approaches to the Communion. A non-dynamic and non-relational thinking about Anglican identity leads to a structural/instrumental approach to the relationship between unity and authority. This has significantly contributed to the fragmentation and polarization seen in situations of conflict, separating it from the life of the triune God's dynamic relationships which is the source and ground of the life of the Anglican Communion at all levels. In other words, this static thinking creates a static theological climate in its life, thereby predefining and polarising the issue of homosexuality, creating a barrier between parties and individuals in the Anglican Communion.

When Anglican identity is understood as a communion, the Anglican Communion has the confidence in that it is called to be a dynamic, relational, and transforming "Church," as opposed to a tribal "church." It becomes one which reflects the life of the triune God's dynamic relationships. Accordingly, the centrality of the life of Anglican identity as Communion allows the Anglican Communion to hold to its inclusive attitude towards differences within the Communion. It can also be open to God's final purpose of embracing all creation in the world. In other words, a new way of thinking about Anglican identity as Communion allows the Communion to create a hospitable and open space for one another. This might create new opportunities for differences in understanding among Anglicans, and thus could transcend the boundaries created by static thinking and thus provide another way forward from the current deadlock.

References

Best, Thomas F. and Gassmann, Günter (eds.), *Official Report of the Fifth World Conference on Faith and Order: On the Way to Fuller Koinonia* (Geneva: WCC Publications, 1994).

Bosch, David J., *Transforming Mission: Paradigm Shifts in Theology of Mission* (Maryknoll, New York: Orbis Books, 1991).

Fiddes, Paul S., *Participating in God: A Pastoral Doctrine of the Trinity* (London: Darton, Longman and Todd, 2000).

Greenwood, Robin, *Transforming Priesthood: A New Theology of Mission and Ministry* (London: SPCK, 1994).

Mission-Shaped Church: Church Planting and Fresh Expressions of Church in a Changing Context (London: Church House Publishing, 2004).

Rosenthal, James M. and Currie, Nicola (eds.), *The Official Report of the 10th Meeting of the Anglican Consultative Council X, Panama City* (Harrisburg, Pennsylvania: Morehouse Publishing, 1997).

Selby, Peter, *Belonging: Challenge to a Tribal Church* (London: SPCK, 1991).

Sykes, Stephen, Booty, John, and Knight, Jonathan (eds.), *The Study of Anglicanism*, revised edition (London: SPCK; Minneapolis: Fortress Press, 1988).

The Lambeth Conference 1948: The Encyclical Letter from the Bishops; together with Resolutions and Reports (London: SPCK 1948).

The New Revised Standard Version of the Bible © 1989.

The Truth Shall Make You Free: The Lambeth Conference 1988 (London: The Anglican Consultative Council, 1988).

The Windsor Report 2004 of the Lambeth Commission on Communion (Harrisburg, Pennsylvania: Morehouse Publishing, 2004).

Williams, Rowan, *Tokens of Trust: An Introduction to Christian belief* (London: Canterbury Press, 2007).

Zizioulas, John D., *Being as Communion: Studies in Personhood and the Church* (New York: St Vladimir's Seminary Press, 1985).

Articles, journals, papers, theses, and publications

"An Anglican Covenant" <https://www.anglicancommunion.org/theology/doctrine/covenant.aspx 9> [accessed March 2024].

Apostolic Constitution Anglicanorum Coetibus Providing for Personal Ordinariates for Anglicans Entering into Full Communion with the Catholic Church, 09.11.2009 <https://press.vatican.va/content/salastampa/it/bollettino/pubblico/2009/11/09/0696/01642.html [accessed March 2024].

Calvani, Carlos, "The Myth of [the] Anglican Communion," *Journal of Anglican Studies*, vol. 3.2 (December 2005).

Cavanagh, Lorraine, "The Freeing of Anglican Identities," *Theology Wales* (2004).

Church of England bishop says "Anglican experiment is over" https://www.catholicnewsagency.com/news/17493/church-of-england-bishop-says-anglican-experiment-is-over [accessed March 2024].

Douglas, Ian T., "An American Reflects on the Windsor Report," *Journal of Anglican Studies*, vol. 3.2 (December 2005).

———. "Anglicans Gathering for God's Mission: A Missiological Ecclesiology for the Anglican Communion," *Journal of Anglican Studies*, vol. 2.2 (December 2004).

———. "Anglican identity and the *Missio Dei*: Implications for the American Convocation of Churches in Europe," *Anglican Theological Review*, vol. 82, no. 3 (2000)

"Global Anglican Future Conference," <Global Fellowship of Confessing Anglicans - Wikipedia>.

Lewis, Harold T., "Covenant, Contract, and Communion: Reflections on a Post-Windsor Anglicanism," *Anglican Theological Review*, vol. 87, no. 4 (Fall 2005).

Ro, Chul-Lai, "Towards the Renewal of Anglican Identity as Communion: The Relationship of the Trinity, Missio Dei, and Anglican Comprehensiveness" (Ph.D. thesis, Cardiff University, 2009).

Rowan Williams, "The Challenge and Hope of Being an Anglican Today: A Reflection for the Bishops, Clergy and Faithful of the Anglican Communion," *Anglican Communion News Service (ACNS)*, no. 4161 (2006). <http://www.anglicancommunion.org/acns/aricles/41/50/acns4161.cfm> [accessed July 2006]

Strudwick, Vincent, "It's a relationship, not a doctrinal quiz," *Church Times* (7 July 2006)

"The 2006 Kigali Communiqué" <http://www.globalsouthanglican.org/index.php/comments/kigali_communique/> [accessed December 2006].

"The Homepage of GAFCON" <https://www.gafcon.org/> [accessed March 2024].

PART TWO

The Particularity of Anglican Identity and Faith in South Africa

CHAPTER FOUR

Black Faith in White Institutional Space: The Struggle for a Liberating and Liberated Faith

Dr. Thandi Gamedze

Given South Africa's history of colonial and apartheid domination through which the racialization of people was deployed to justify oppression and exploitation, race remains a salient concept today. This history—and the complex ways in which these dynamics persist even after these systems have been "overturned"—has ensured that significant inequality remains, largely along racial lines. Because of this, race cannot be ignored.

This is uniquely true when examining the church, as this institution played a central role in the work of racialization and the subsequent justification of racism and the oppression of Black people in South Africa. Christianity in South Africa cannot be understood outside of its introduction via the broader missionary movement in the eighteenth and nineteenth centuries. Similarly, the colonial project cannot be understood outside of its missionary roots, Comaroff (1989) referring to the missionaries as "the vanguards of empire and its most active ideological agents" (Comaroff, 1989, 663).

Within this, missionaries' ideas about salvation were intertwined with deeply entrenched ideas about race, with

Africans seen as inferior in every way (Cochrane, 1987). This worldview colored and shaped both the rationale and the strategy of the missionary project, legitimizing and even necessitating it. In this worldview, as the superior and more civilized parties, the missionaries saw themselves as carrying a responsibility for ruling and bringing civilization to those they viewed as inferior (Cochrane, 1987). This inherently racist foundation had significant implications for the South African church.

Of course, this history is centuries removed from the church today. However, the various mechanisms upholding the deep racial inequalities that persist in South African society are also operational in the church. As a Black woman, having spent most of my life in South Africa and within various church expressions, my own personal experience can attest to this. These realities have been reflected, too, over the years in numerous conversations with friends. I have also spent seven years working for an Anglican parish-birthed ecumenical organization dedicated to supporting and equipping churches to be peace and justice makers in the world, and in this work have time and time again come face to face with areas in which churches are failing to do this work of justice, for purposes of this chapter, particularly as it relates to race.

More recently, I have seen and analysed some of these realities empirically through my PhD research. In this, I made use of the extended case method[1] to examine the mechanisms

---

1. This method "applies reflexive science to ethnography in order to extract the general from the unique, to move from the 'micro' to the 'macro,' and to connect the present to the past in anticipation of the future, all by building on preexisting theory" (Burawoy, 1998, 5).

through which Meeting Point[2], a Pentecostal Charismatic Evangelical (PCE)[3] congregation based in a historically White suburb in Cape Town, establishes and maintains White dominance and Black inferiority. The research was ethnographic in nature and involved attending and observing church services, attending and observing "life groups" (small groups of around ten people who meet weekly to discuss the previous sermon among other things), studying and analysing church sermons and church documents, and interviewing congregants past and present. Notably, while this was a case study of one specific congregation, the congregation in question is one of eleven in the Western Cape under the same church umbrella. Additionally, it is a member of a global network of churches aligned in their doctrine, structures, and practices. Thus, while I do not make overt claims to reproducibility of findings, significant similarities across these churches are likely. Additionally, from my own lifetime of experience with churches of all kinds, I can attest that these dynamics exist—albeit in varying ways—beyond this defined scope.

This chapter will go on to draw on this research to provide a description and analysis of the ways that White dominance persists and is reinscribed within the realm of Meeting Point. It will then explore the dilemma that this poses for Black people

---

2. Meeting Point is a pseudonym.

3. A classification coined by Frahm-Arp (2015). She explains that although the Pentecostal, Evangelical, and Charismatic movements historically had different origins and markers, in the contemporary church this has become far more fluid, and over time there has been significant cross-pollination between movements. For this reason, Pentecostal Charismatic Evangelical (PCE) is a useful categorization for churches fitting somewhere within this spectrum.

and their faith within the church. Finally, drawing on both the testimonies of Black people within these church realities, as well as histories of those who have navigated similar faith dynamics, the chapter will explore the ways in which Black people navigate White institutional Christianity to carve out paths for liberating and liberated faith.

Before I get into that, a quick disclaimer. In writing a piece which uses race as a central analytical concept, I want to ensure that I am not reproducing "racialized forms of consciousness" (Vally & Motala, 2018, 39) through "an uncritical acceptance of apartheid racial categories" (Vally & Motala, 2018, 31). As scholars of critical race theory teach, race is a social construction created and employed for the purposes of oppression and exploitation (Ladson-Billings, 2022), yet because of the systems built around this social construct (particularly that of racial capitalism upon which colonialism and apartheid in South Africa were built), race continues to carry political, social, and economic relevance in society (Soudien, 2013).

In order to walk the line of recognizing the sociopolitical importance of race, but taking care to problematize it, Vally and Motala argue that distinctions must be made "between racism as social explanation and race as simply an uncritical acceptance of apartheid racial categories" (Vally & Motala, 2018, 31). Again, critical race theorists walk this line through focusing their attention on the mechanisms through which race "gets made and remade" (Montgomery, 2005, 319). This is how I have attempted to approach this next section.

How the White institutional space is set up and its characteristics

Moore's (2020) conception of White institutional space (WIS) is useful in thinking about how institutions perpetuate and sustain dominant racial power dynamics. Using elite law schools in the United States (US) as a case, Moore demonstrates the ways in which "organizations... are produced by and function to reproduce racialized social institutions... and therefore reify the racial social structure" (Moore, 2020, 1946). Moore describes such organizations as "White institutional spaces" and explores both the tacit and explicit mechanisms through which such spaces reproduce White privilege and power. This section will make visible some of the mechanisms through which Meeting Point functions as a WIS.

Dynamics of institutional power

In theorising how law schools in the US sustain and reproduce White supremacy, Moore (2020) argues that "White space not only relies on who is or is not in law schools, but more important, who has institutional power within those schools" (Moore, 2020, 1955).

Despite Meeting Point's White majority membership, there is a measure of racial diversity within the congregation. However, notably, this diversity does not extend to either Meeting Point's speakers, leadership structures, or the thinkers and theologians drawn from in church teachings. A tiny minority of sermons observed were preached by people of color. Black people are severely underrepresented when it comes to who is permitted to authoritatively speak in the church. This dynamic is reflected, too, in the church's leadership structures in that the eldership team of the church is solely made up of White men.[4] Moore emphasizes that these kinds of "racialized patterns of institutional power create tacit institutional meanings" (Ibid., 1956) which naturalize and normalize (and in the church context, even sacralize) White power. Similar patterns of White (and Western) dominance are evidenced in the thinkers and theologians drawn from in sermon content. In my observations, none of the theologians referenced within Meeting Point's sermons were people of color. All were White, and aside from two South Africans, all were from either Europe or the US.

This kind of deference to the West and to Whiteness has a long history, specifically within the Christian tradition. Jennings (2020), writing about theological education in the US context describes this as "the tragic history of Christians who came not to learn anything from indigenous peoples but only to instruct them, and to exorcise and eradicate anything and everything that seemed strange and therefore anti-Christian" (Jennings 2020, 40). The persistence of this dynamic—the centering of Western knowledge and the marginalization of that which is indigenous— is a central concern of decoloniality scholarship. Heleta (2021) argues that "despite the end of apartheid in 1994, Eurocentric knowledge, rooted in colonial and apartheid education, remains

---

4. For the initial part of the period over which I was observing church services, there was one person of color on the eldership team. However, this was short-lived and "hermeneutical differences" was cited as the reason for his stepping down from eldership.

the norm, displacing all other knowledges, epistemologies, and schools of thought" (Heleta 2021, 182). Such tendencies are very present within Meeting Point, as well as other churches within South Africa, and tacitly maintain White supremacy and reproduce WIS through centering White, Western knowledge. Through this, such knowledge is naturalized and normalized and "bolstered by a narrative of objectivity and impartiality" (Moore 2020, 1956)— with significant implications.

Discursive (lack of) engagement with race

Another "principal mechanism of contemporary White institutional space" (Moore 2020, 1955) is the ignoring and avoidance of the salience of race or the historical mechanisms through which it is created. This is a reality within Meeting Point's discourse.

In my analysis, direct engagement with and naming of race was all but absent in sermon messaging. Instead, terms like "unity," "differences," "different cultures," "inclusive," and "no demographic requirement" appeared to be used as proxies for making reference to race. At times, biblical language was also drawn from, with ideas such as "every nation and tribe and people and tongue" (Revelation 7:9) used to touch on these topics.

This unwillingness to overtly name and address race was even present within an official Meeting Point document written to guide the church's response to this topic. Instead of naming race, the document is nebulously titled *Diversity and Human Relations* (Meeting Point 2019). While this document represents the church's most overt attempt to address issues of race, the hesitancy to clearly name this is present here too. The language of "ethnicity," "culture," "heritage," and "identity" are frequently used as proxies for race. Racism is largely talked about as "ethnic intolerance," "prejudice," "prejudicial actions and attitudes," "prejudicial attitudes, beliefs, and behavior." Finally, the antithesis to racism and racist behaviour is portrayed in the document as "unity," "reconciliation," "peace," "diversity," "ethnic inclusion," "radical inclusion" or being "ethnicity-and-culture-affirming" (Meeting Point 2019).

Notable to this conversation, Han (2009), in her work on Korean churches in the US, details how the avoidance of references to race "and opting instead for ethnicity and language. . . attempts to depoliticize what is actually a variation of racial taxonomy project" (Han 2009, 49). Montgomery (2005) makes a similar argument. In his analysis of Canadian history textbooks, he finds that "categories such as origin, ethnicity and descent" (Montgomery 2005, 334) are used to speak about race in ways that appear neutral, yet due to their preoccupation "with human typology" (Ibid.) act to perpetuate racialized and racist realities. Soudien argues similarly, and refers to these as "alibi concepts"—concepts which continue to "do the work of race," implicitly perpetuating "racial biology as an explanation of how 'race' works" (Soudien 2013).

In Apple's words, these tactics of avoidance and sidestepping ensure that race remains "the absent presence whose overt absence masks its power in our daily lives" (Apple 2006, 164). Through this masking, the racial inequalities still so pervasive in South African society remain protected and untouched and continue to be reproduced.

Colorblindness

Another related way in which WIS is perpetuated is through the "use of "discursive storylines that equate equality with treating all individuals the same, while ignoring racial differences resulting from contemporary racial hierarchy or the history of White supremacy" (Moore 2020, 1955). This is also known as colorblindness, or colorblind racism.

This dynamic, too, is present within Meeting Point. The church, despite being majority White in a majority Black country, portrays itself as an inclusive community in which "anyone can walk through those doors on a Sunday, and. . . be welcomed" (Sermon 06/03/2022). This narrative is reinforced with the argument that at Meeting Point, "there's no entry fee, no annual membership, no demographic requirement, no qualifying factors" (Sermon 06/03/2022). Such a narrative claims equality while erasing the realities of how race functions (materially as well as ontologically) in South African society to exclude Black people from White institutional spaces like Meeting Point. In short, there is a clear obscuring of the systems and structures rooted in histories of racial capitalism which perpetuate unequal racialized realities.

Notably, such ideologies are legitimized scripturally and thereby sacralized. In Curtis' work on White evangelicalism in the US, he notes that, "though White evangelicals alone did not create the politics of colorblindness, tens of millions of White evangelicals drew on their theology to imbue those politics with a sacred character" (Curtis 2019, 6). In Meeting Point, this happens through the appropriation of biblically inspired ideas such as "unity in Christ" (Meeting Point 2019, 18), or the erasure of any differences between members because they have "Jesus in common" (Sermon 06/03/2022), which functions in tandem with the idea that a person's Christian identity supersedes their racial identity.

Framing racism as interpersonal

Another way in which the systems which perpetuate racial inequality are obscured, and thus WIS perpetuated, is through the individualization of issues around race. Racism, instead of being understood as structural, systemic, and institutional, is individualized and limited to the realm of interpersonal attitudes and behaviour.

This happens within Meeting Point through an articulated desire for and prioritization of "unity," "diversity," and "reconciliation," devoid of efforts to address this at its roots, or engagement with the material barriers to it. The only actions suggested to achieve this vision of an inclusive, diverse, and united church include prayer (Sermon 06/03/2022) and congregants changing who they sit with, eat with, live with, etc., to ensure that they are creating spaces of diversity in their own lives and not just doing life with people who "look like," "talk like" or "dress like" them (Sermon 06/03/2022).

This echoes a tendency found within White evangelicalism to stress "the importance of interpersonal relationships to heal the wounds of racism" (Curtis 2019, 3). Such a positioning fails to acknowledge the structural and systemic ways that racial patterns continue to inscribe themselves and forecloses space for engagement with the kinds of actions required to address these systemic issues. Instead, symptoms are separated from their root causes, while the issue is individualized and removed from any of its economic and structural implications.

The *Diversity and Human Relations* document continues along these individualistic lines and adds a spiritual element. The document argues that "it is sin that has broken down human relationships, and therefore the work of Christ in believers' hearts will bring about a gospel-infused honor for all others" (Meeting Point 2019, 3), and that "ethnic differences can be overcome by the work of Christ" (Ibid., 4). The document in fact goes as far as to say that "*only* the gospel has the power to transform people's hearts from hatred to respect, honor and love" (Ibid., 7, emphasis mine). In addition, rather than addressing the systemic and structural issues, the document positions the solution as, among other things, "greater depths of understanding and application" of "diversity and reconciliation," "cross-cultural relationships," "unity in diversity," "honor(ing) each other, and valuing our ethnic differences," personally repenting, and "seeking forgiveness for sinning against your "brother or sister" (Ibid., 7). This not only works to individualize and personalize systemic and structural issues, but it also spiritualizes issues that are very much material.

Such a tendency is by no means new. In fact, it has glaring parallels to aspects of the 1985 Kairos Document, a document written in the height of apartheid repression as a challenge to the South African church which was perceived to be failing to in its response to this context. The document describes what it refers to as "church theology," at the heart of which it argues is a "reliance upon 'individual conversions' in response to 'moralising demands' to change the structures of a society" (Kairos 1985, 17). Yet, as the document surmises, it is no less true today than it was then that "the problem that we are dealing with here in South Africa is not merely a problem of personal guilt, it is a problem of structural injustice" (Ibid.).

Limits on Black participation

Notably, WIS does not require an absence of Black people— in fact, for the purposes of legitimacy, it often requires the presence of Black people in some shape or form. However, WIS enacts various forms of disciplinary power to control which Black people can be present and how they should behave in the space. Along these lines, in writing from a US context, Bracey (2016) argues that White evangelical churches construct semipermeable racial boundaries which work to maintain "a delicate balance between ensuring the continuation of White spaces and having enough visible minorities to defend against charges of racism" (Bracey 2016, 72). Bracey continues to argue that "White evangelicals work to be sure only a few people of color enter their churches and that those few are the 'right kind of people.'" (Ibid., 74).

A similar dynamic at Meeting Point was revealed by one participant in reflecting upon the predominantly White state of the church:

When you plant a church, and one hundred percent or ninety. . . plus percent of the people are White, it was an actual decision. It wasn't circumstance, it was a proper decision, right? Because you're in South Africa. . . So now how do you reverse something that is 20 years old? . . . You just can't. That church will forever be a White church. . . or if it's not going to be White, it's going to be reaching specific types of Black people. (Interview 26/07/2023)

This idea of "specific types of Black people" (Ibid.) or what Bracey (2016) refers to as "the right kind of (Black) people" (Bracey 2016, 74) is important in WIS. Bracey (2016) argues that such people are those who do not "disrupt the norms of religious White space" (Ibid., 74) and who are willing to use their racial status to "serve the church's perceived racial needs" (Bracey 2016, 88). In line with this, the participant says the following: "There's specific Black people like myself who survived in that space for six years. And not every Black person is gonna survive in that space. I could, right? So you're gonna get specific types of Black people in that space." (Interview 26/07/2023)

Already a congregant at the church and in good relationship with the church leaders, the participant details how, upon seeing some of things that he was involved in outside of the church including various artistic pursuits, the church leaders invited him onto staff to join the leadership team. This intentional recruitment of certain people of color is also evidenced another participant's story. She explains how she and her husband joined the church, "then, soon, people discovered our gifting and who we were and what we were capable of doing" (Interview, 10/03/2023). Following this, they were recruited into the church's ministry and then onto the church's leadership team.

Bracey (2016) makes an important contribution in his theorization of what he terms "race tests" as a central mechanism through which White evangelical churches ensure the maintenance of WIS (Bracey 2016). Bracey distinguishes between exclusionary race tests and utility-based race tests, arguing that the former seek to eradicate Black people whose politics, thought, or presence would disrupt the White institutional space, whereas the latter seek to recruit "assimilable persons of color" (Bracey 2016, 88) who will "serve the church's perceived racial needs" (Ibid., 88). Parallels between Meeting Point and Bracey's assessment of the US-based White evangelical churches that he studies are clear in that the recruitment of the interviewees mentioned appeared to be based on their skills, talents, and capabilities and how those would serve the church.

Related to this the WIS also places—largely unspoken—limits on how people of color should behave and respond, particularly to issues around race. Black people—unsurprisingly—feel the need to address incidents of racism, yet bear the burden of doing so without posing a threat to the WIS. The following narrative illustrates this, while also showing how some of the church's official discourse prioritizing narratives of unity and reconciliation, and framing racism and its solutions as interpersonal, becomes internalized by and disciplines the subjectivities of congregants of color. One participant told a story of how, over the time of the KwaZulu Natal (KZN) and Gauteng "unrest" in July 2021, one of the people in her life group posted a racist meme on the life group's WhatsApp group.

Within the group, one of the members challenged this message, and this led to the group having a conversation about it (Interview 9/10/2021). The participant was glad to have the conversation but said that it was quite awkward (partly because it happened on Zoom) and the leaders of the life group—a White couple—seemed out of their depth. Her commentary on the situation largely aligned to the church's ideas about unity and reconciliation: "So that was a very interesting. . . racial dynamic, that we needed to have hard conversations, whether it would offend. . . but we really needed to navigate it together and kind of talk things through—why this is not right, and why it's offensive to some people. And then to be able to keep doing life together thereafter." (Interview 9/10/2021)

Here, the participant—a person of color—was hesitant to say anything too harsh about the person who had sent the meme, or the meme itself. She did not say that the meme was racist— just that it was offensive and had "racial profiling connotations" (Ibid.). In addition, she was lenient towards the person who had posted the meme, implying that they may not have understood why the meme was not right and why it might be offensive. She also framed the work of explaining this to the person as her (and others in the life group's) responsibility. The participant also expects and plays into "White fragility"[5] (DiAngelo 2011),

_____

5. DiAngelo characterizes White fragility as "the reduced psychosocial stamina that racial insulation inculcates" in people racialized as "White" (DiAngelo 2011, 56). This state results from a social environment of "racial protection" which "builds White expectations for racial comfort while at the

worrying that such a conversation "would offend" (Ibid.) others. Importantly, in her assessment, the outcome of the conversation should be to "keep doing life together thereafter" (Interview 9/10/2021). This is a significant burden that Black people in the space must carry. They must address racism, but in a way that does not offend the people who display it. They must explain to people why racism is not right and why it is offensive. Finally, they must continue to "do life" with or be reconciled to the people who have been perpetuating the racism.

Summary so far

In the myriad ways described above, in line with Moore's (2020) theorization about White institutional space and how this is sustained and perpetuated through Meeting Point's "discourse, ideology, practice, and hierarchies of power" (Moore 2020, 1955), White power and privilege is reified, naturalized, and even sacralized within the space. Through various mechanisms, racial hierarchy organized around a structure of White supremacy, is upheld and reproduced. These mechanisms include "racialized patterns of institutional power" (Moore 2020, 1956), "the de-politicization of power relations," (Araújo & Maeso 2012, 1267), the hesitancy to name and address issues of race, the framing of racism and its solutions as interpersonal and requiring of "individual conversions" rather than structural solutions, the centering of concepts such as unity and reconciliation devoid

---

same time lowering the ability to tolerate racial stress" (Ibid., 54). This all functions to "reinstate White racial equilibrium." (Ibid.).

of concrete reparations, as well as the disciplinary mechanisms enacted by the WIS, which determine which Black people are welcomed into the space and how they should behave.

Black and Christian: the dilemma

Throughout Christianity's history, largely because of its deep entanglement with stories of empire, colonization, enslavement, and domination, the faith has posed a dilemma for the dominated. This was true for enslaved Africans in the United States who embraced Christianity. In writing about the dilemmas introduced by the dynamics of Christianity as the religion of the master and then being taken up by the enslaved, Carter (2007) frames American evangelicalism as "a movement with a crisis in its very heart."

It was true for Black evangelicals in the US who found themselves within the White evangelical church. Sharp describes the dilemma of Black people faced with the inherent racism of the evangelical church and faith that came with the realization "that what they thought was an evangelical view of the world was in fact a White evangelical view of the world" (Sharp 2018).

It was true also for Black South African Christians under apartheid rule. Mofokeng (1987) articulates this dilemma from this context of severe oppression and domination, saying: "We also worship—many of us—in churches wherein the same relations of White domination and ruthless brutalization of Black Christians are reproduced" (Mofokeng 1987). Mofokeng recognizes that within the church, this domination happens not only materially as in the rest of society, but also theologically.

He notes that this situation poses a fundamental dilemma "for those Black Christians who. . . still want to retain their faith in Jesus the Messiah."

In contemporary South Africa, thirty years post-apartheid, the dilemma for Black Christians—specifically in churches complicit in reproducing White domination—remains. The at best uncomfortable and at worst violent reality of WIS enacts itself in various ways upon Black bodies. My interviews with Black participants revealed the numerous challenges that they have faced as this WIS forecloses certain possibilities, forcing Black people to inhabit certain subjectivities. These realities present a dilemma of faith for Black congregants at Meeting Point.

One participant, in unpacking some of her thought processes at the time, particularly as they relate to the failure of the church to address racial injustice both internally and externally, described her dilemma as follows: "I love how you guys (referring to those at the church) love Jesus. But I also don't understand how you guys love Jesus and it's not clicking for you. And your church looks like this" (Interview 18/05/2023).

She simultaneously holds an admiration for the faith of those she sees at the church, and is shocked and disappointed that this faith appears to have little to say about racial injustice inside or outside of the church. She laments the failure of this faith to translate into transformative justice-seeking action. She laments that this faith—at least at it is expressed within Meeting Point—is complicit in her own oppression as a Black person. She describes the impact of such a reality on her faith: "I think there is something that erodes even your own relationship with God when you are in a position where you're constantly having to correct, you know, where you're constantly sitting, and you are critical" (Interview 18/05/2023). This is the dilemma of coming face to face with the reality of being a Black person who has embraced a faith which for all intents and purposes appears to be in favor of your continued dehumanization and diminishment. One questions whether these two identities— that of being Black and that of being Christian—are in fact reconcilable. This dilemma parallels with Du Bois' articulation of that of being both Black and American: 'There is within and without the sound of conflict, the burning of body and rending of soul; inspiration strives with doubt, and faith with vain questionings" (Du Bois 2007, 13).

Responses to the dilemma: avoidance, acceptance, and compartmentalization

People respond to this dilemma in a myriad of ways. One such response—or perhaps more accurately, non-response—may be characterized as avoidance. A participant recounts her experience at the church of Black people who refuse to see or engage with this dilemma— whether consciously or not—and thus don't overtly desire or make attempts to see change. Within this, she describes such people's unwillingness to enter conversations that seek to highlight, disturb, or challenge the racial status quo: "They don't understand that. . . this is not okay. . . Like we've kind of accepted the status quo. 'I'm just coming to church on a Sunday. Please don't involve me in your chats.' Because also their lives are very separate." (Interview 18/05/2023)

Others, perhaps for their own sanity and survival in the face of the improbability of change, consciously compartmentalize their Blackness from their White institutional Christianity. This is described by one participant below:

> Let's say, someone like me. . . You're really passionate and you feel a call to serve in the local church. And so, once you get into that space, you put ideology aside, because. . . . it's gonna take many years. . . it's not gonna take a book, it's not going to take me sitting down and explaining racism and power structures, and whatever. . . all of this stuff is just not gonna work. And so, you just realize, okay, let me rather swim in the stream—or let me just get out. (Interview 26/07/2023)

This kind of forced compartmentalization hearkens back to Du Bois' ideas around double consciousness (Du Bois 2007). He describes a "two-ness,—an American (or in our case, a Christian), a Negro; two souls, two thoughts, two unreconciled strivings; two warring ideals in one dark body, whose dogged strength alone keeps it from being torn asunder." (Du Bois 2007, 8).

The participant's reflections demonstrate the warring and irreconcilable nature of the strivings of the Black person and the Christian, both held within one body. Here, putting ideology aside essentially translates to putting one's Blackness aside. Hence, if one chooses to remain in the church and keep this particular faith, one's Blackness cannot be part of it.

Urbaniak (2019) similarly draws on this idea of double consciousness in reflecting on the fallist student movements.[6] He notes that despite the recognition that the majority of #RhodesMustFall (#RMF) supporters on the ground were on the Christian spectrum (Chikane 2018), there is a lack of explicit reference to religion within fallist scholarship (Urbaniak 2019). Urbaniak concludes (perhaps contestably) that this implies a "silence about Christianity within the movement" (Urbaniak 2019, 228), perhaps indicating a recognition by students that, at least in the quest for decolonization and other goals of the fallist movement, "Christianity is part of the problem, rather than the solution" (Ibid.). In this choice to compartmentalize their faith from their Black aspirations for freedom, Urbaniak describes what he imagines in the students as a "schizophrenic split between their Christian and their African identities" (Urbaniak 2019, 232).

This dynamic was similarly reflected by Mosala (2021), in describing the ways in which Black students at seminaries in the 1970s during the rise of Black consciousness (BC) struggled to negotiate their Blackness and their Christianity (Mosala 2021). He describes the moment as follows: "Campuses were on fire, Black students were revolting against anything and everything colonial" (Mosala 2021). Noting the "racism and racialism that happens inside of the churches," students recognized that their faith and the then current church expressions of it were very

---

6. This refers to the #RhodesMustFall and #FeesMustFall movements that took place in 2015 and 2016 in several South African universities where demands were made for, among other things, the decolonization of universities and their curricula (both overt and hidden).

much included in the category of "anything and everything colonial" (Ibid.).

The tension evoked by such disjuncture is again reminiscent of Du Bois' cry:

Why did God make me an outcast and a stranger in mine own house? (Du Bois 2007, 8)

This cry captures the deep tensions emerging as a result of being Black in WIS. Black people are forced into certain limited subjectivities. One has the choice of either putting one's "ideology aside" (Interview 26/07/2023) and swimming in the stream, getting out of the stream altogether, or signing up for the hard and often frustrating work of attempting to reconcile the contradictions of the double consciousness by resisting the structures that reproduce and reinscribe WIS, and appropriating or reclaiming one's faith to transform it into that which is both liberated and liberating. The latter will be explored below.

Resistance and reclaiming

For interviewee 8, the consciousness of the disjuncture between her faith and her Blackness led to robust engagement to successfully combat what had felt like an irreconcilable disequilibrium—what Vellem (2018) refers to as "the dilemma of merging the contradictions of a double-self syndrome resulting from Black self and Christianity" (Vellem 2018, 276).

In one participant's reflections, it appears that some, like her, succeed in reconciling their Blackness with their Christianity, and from this position find it hard to understand how "it's not clicking" (Interview 18/05/2023) for others. In this, there is an implicit assumption that Christianity should imply some level of desire and advocacy for racial justice. Within White institutional spaces, Black people often end up becoming the advocates for this change.

For part of the period that I was observing church services, there was one person of color on the eldership team. In my experience at the church, he was the one of two people that spoke about anything to do with race and social justice. On the church service that fell on Human Rights Day, he referenced the Sharpeville Massacre and some related South African history in his prayer (CS Observations 21/03/2021). He also led the prayer at the service around the time of the "unrest" in KZN and Gauteng (CS Observations 18/07/2021). Additionally, he preached one sermon in which he spoke quite extensively about social justice (CS Observations 04/07/2021).

During the period of my observations, the one other time that someone spoke about social justice in a sermon, it was also a person of color (CS Observation 03/04/2022). At the very least, this is an interesting observation, and raises questions around whether this is intentional (a move to create some form of legitimacy to a racial demographic in which White people predominate), or simply happens because Black people are not able to ignore these issues and thus they emerge when they speak, while White people are much more able to ignore them.

This dynamic was also present in one participant's reflections, where, in her time at the church, a significant aspect of her identity and role was related to educating people about race: "I was involved in every conversation, workshop about race." (Interview 18/05/2023) This was also reflected in her smaller scale interactions where she became the go-to person for White congregants trying to understand or deal with race-related matters: 'I become this Black girl who, if you want to talk about issues of race, if you want to talk about what is happening on campus (regarding #RMF and #FMF), and get an understanding what's happening, I'm the go-to person. (Interview 18/05/2023)

In this, she not only had to deal with the dynamics of what it means to be a Black person in a space whose teachings and practices endorse and perpetuate Whiteness (WIS), she was also burdened with the weighty task of eradicating racism in the church. This burden is well captured in the story recounted here: "I remember after doing a workshop on race at. . . a church camp, or church getaway, there was a White boy who came up to me and asked me to pray with him because he was struggling with racism. It was the most absurd thing in my life. (Interview 18/05/2023)

Another participant's experience speaks to a similar dynamic. She recounts joining the church. Once her and her husband's giftings were discovered, in part due to the kind of feedback they would give to the elders, they were tasked with starting Meeting Point's social justice ministry. This was in part precipitated by #RMF and #FMF: "That kind of nudged into us really having hard conversations. . . So, we were the team organising those kinds of things. To create more social awareness, we had some events on higher education and injustice. And that then morphed into what they call the social justice ministry." (Interview 10/03/2023)

This dynamic is not a new one. Sharp (2018) details the emergence of "the radical Black evangelical movement of the late 1960s and 1970s" (in the US) as "a direct response to their disillusioning experiences in a predominantly White evangelical subculture" (Sharp 2018, 2). The fallist student movements emerged from similar "disillusioning experiences" of Black students with exclusionary colonial institutional structures and realities. What is perhaps different in these church experiences however, particularly those of one participant, is that this "conscientizing" work is often done alone and not as part of any organized grouping or movement. Looking back at these experiences, she reflects on the toll that they took: "I look back at those years and. . . I mourn my late teens and my early twenties, because I was way too young, way too young to be navigating those things. I was way too young to have felt like the burden of change at (the church) was on me. And I was way too young to be teaching grownups." (Interview 10/03/2023)

The response to the hostility of WIS often involves Black people finding or creating safe spaces for themselves within the environment. One of these safe spaces for the same participant was the church's tutoring program in Langa—a nearby township—which she somewhat jokingly describes as "Black work": "Those are kind of like the White people that I. . . kind of feel safe with because we're doing "Black work." (Interview 10/03/2023)

Where safe spaces are non-existent, Black people create them for themselves. This participant speaks about her efforts to create this kind of community for Black women in the church. Becoming a life group leader was a turning point for her in this regard. Previously, as a way of responding to other dynamics of

WIS, she had intentionally refrained from forming friendships with other Black people in the space, but taking on this position instilled in her a feeling of responsibility to do the opposite: "I was like, okay, cool, I guess I can't not be friends with Black people now because. . . I have a responsibility. . . And so like. . . on Sundays, I would actually reach out to a whole lot of Black people, Black girls in particular." (Interview 10/03/2023)

This took the shape of both a space of conscientization ("on the side there, I was definitely conscientising people" [Ibid.]) as well as a space of community and solidarity ("I had. . . created a little community of Black girls at [the church] and we were like, kind of friends and sisters. And we would check up on each other" [Ibid.]).

Another participant recounts her efforts to do similar work in creating spaces for conversations about race. She recalls organising and hosting an event engaging with some of the themes emerging from the Black Panther movie, as well as various other events, conversations, and discussions around social justice issues.

One participant, recalling of her interactions with a fellow Black person in the church around the time of George Floyd's murder in the US, also shows how current events (in that example, the murder of George Floyd) can also precipitate networks of solidarity between people of color. For this person, this event seemed to represent something of a wakeup call in regard to his own Blackness within a WIS.

In the ways described above, the disillusionment emerging from the hostility of White institutional spaces towards Black people, often results in Black people either seeking out the marginal spaces of safety within these environments or creating such spaces for themselves.

Finally, at times, the work of resistance to colonial appropriations of Christianity and the reclaiming of Black faith at times involves breaking ties with WIS. Significantly, most of the people of color whose interviews make up the substance of this chapter are no longer at Meeting Point. The reasons for this are different, but each of them expressed some level of frustration with the unchanging nature of racial dynamics at the church, despite having spent significant energy and resource towards the hoped-for change. As alluded to by one participant, this frustration often comes when there have been certain (perceived) commitments to change, but these simply do not materialize: "I think. . . my frustration is that like, you guys (referring to the elders) get it. We've spoken about this. And you guys have a plan towards this. But then. . . you know what I mean? Like, it's like, why are. . . there more White elders that are being added into the into the team? Like, I don't understand." (Interview 18/05/2023)

In some—as in the case of another participant—this frustration becomes a kind of resignation to what is perceived as the inevitability of the White institutional space: "So now how do you reverse something that is 20 years old? . . . You just can't. That church will forever be a White church." (Interview 26/07/2023). In light of such a conclusion, when all attempts to bring change fail, breaking ties with such institutions is perhaps the most decisive, logical, and expedient pathway to reclaiming Black faith.

Conclusion

This chapter has explored how Christianity and its expressions across contexts—both historical and contemporary—have alienated and subjugated Black people in a myriad of ways. It has also discussed the various mechanisms through which, in these same contexts, this colonial imagination of Christianity has been resisted and Black faith reclaimed. In the South African context, as well as beyond, our history is replete with these stories of faith reclamation. However, these are histories that are often hidden, and removed from the ambit of those fighting similar battles to reclaim their faith today.

Given the realities discussed in this chapter faced by many Black Christians in South Africa (and elsewhere), it would of course be wonderful if churches whose theology, discourse, and practices uphold White institutional space would repent of this, renounce it, and take radical material steps towards creating something different. However, failing this, Black faith, as it always has, will live on. Whether WIS takes heed or not, is, in a certain way, inconsequential. It is time we as Black Christians take matters into our own hands as many of our ancestors have done before us and employ deep and intentional praxes to not only reject the colonial Christianities that represent such a dilemma for our combined Black and Christian identities, but also (perhaps even more crucially) do the faithful work to build and fight for a faith that is both liberated and liberating for all who are oppressed.

References

Apple, M. W., *Educating the "Right" Way: Markets, Standards, God, and Inequality* (2006, Second). Routledge. https://doi .org/10.1177/0973184913411215

Araújo, M., & Maeso, S. R., History textbooks, racism and the critique of Eurocentrism: Beyond rectification or compensation. *Ethnic and Racial Studies*, 35(7), 1266–1286. https://doi.org/10.1080 /01419870.2011.600767

Bracey, G. E., *The White Evangelical Church: White Evangelicalism as a Racial Social Movement* (Issue August, 2016).

Burawoy, M., "The Extended Case Method." *Sociological Theory*, 16(1), 4–33. https://doi.org/10.1111/0735-2751.00040,

Chikane, R., *Breaking A Rainbow, Building A Nation: The Politics Behind #MustFall Movements*, 2018.

Cochrane, J., *Servants of Power: The role of English-speaking Churches 1903–1930*. Raven Press,1987.

Comaroff, J. L., "Images of empire, contests of conscience: Models of colonial domination in South Africa." *American Ethnologist*, 1989, 661–685.

Curtis, J. N., *Colorblind Christians: White Evangelical Institutions and Theologies of Race in the Era of Civil Rights. PhD diss, Temple University*, 2019.

DiAngelo, R., "White Fragility: Why It's so Hard for White People to Talk about Racism." *International Journal of Critical Pedagogy*, 3(3). https://doi.org/10.1080/2194587x.2019.1591288

Du Bois, W. E. B., *The Souls of Black Folk*. Oxford University Press, 2007.

Han, J. H. J., *Contemporary Korean/American Evangelical Missions: Politics of Space, Gender and Difference*. https://escholarship.org /uc/item/4hr8c2ft

Heleta, S., "Coloniality, knowledge production, and racialized socio-economic inequality in South Africa." In M. E. Ruprecht Fadem & M. O'Sullivan (Eds.), *The Economics of Empire: Genealogies of Capital and the Colonial Encounter*. Routledge, 2021.

Jennings, W. J., *After Whiteness: An Education in Belonging*. William B. Eerdmans.

Kairos. (1985). Challenge to the Church: The Kairos Document. In *The Kairos Documents*, Vol. 53, 2020.

Ladson-Billings, G., "Just What Is Critical Race Theory and What's It Doing in a Nice Field Like Education?" In E. Taylor, D. Gillborn, & G. Ladson-Billings (Eds.), *Foundations of Critical Race Theory in Education* (Third). Routledge, 2022.

Montgomery, K., "Banal Race-thinking: Ties of blood, Canadian history textbooks and ethnic nationalism." *Paedagogica Historica*, *41*(3), 313–336. https://doi.org/10.1080/00309230500069795

Moore, W. L., The Mechanisms of White Space(s). *American Behavioral Scientist*, *64*(14), 1946–1960. https://doi.org/10.1177/0002764220975080

Sharp, I., "Diagnosing an 'Unholy Alliance': The Radical Black Evangelical Critique of White Evangelical Nationalism." *Black Theology Papers*, *4*(1), 1–7.

Soudien, C., "'Race' and Its Contemporary Confusions: Towards a Re-statement." *Theoria*, *60*(136), 15–37. https://doi.org/10.3167/th.2013.6013603

Urbaniak, J., "Decolonization as Unlearning Christianity: Fallism and African Religiosity as Case Studies." *Black Theology*, *17*(3), 223–240. https://doi.org/10.1080/14769948.2019.1688088

Vally, S., & Motala, E., "Troubling 'race' as a category of explanation in social science research and analysis." *Southern Africa Review of Education*, *24*(1), 25–42. https://hdl.handle.net/10520/EJC-15ad80d3a2

Vellem, V. S., "Cracking the eurocentric code a battle on the banks of the 'new blood rivers.'" *Missionalia*, *46*(2), 267–287. https://doi .org/10.7832/46-2-313

Church Documents

Meeting Point (2019). Diversity and Human Relations.

Church Sermons

Meeting Point (2022). Sermon 06/03/2022

Participant Interviews

Interviewee 1 (2021). Interviewed by Thandi Gamedze. 09/10/2021, Cape Town, South Africa

Interviewee 2 (2021). Interviewed by Thandi Gamedze. 10/03/2023, Online

Interviewee 3 (2021). Interviewed by Thandi Gamedze. 18/05/2023, Online

Interviewee 4 (2021). Interviewed by Thandi Gamedze. 26/07/2023, Online

Church Service Observations

Fieldnotes from church service observations (21/03/2021)
Fieldnotes from church service observations (18/07/2021)
Fieldnotes from church service observations (04/07/2021)
Fieldnotes from church service observations (03/04/2022)

CHAPTER FIVE

Anglicanism, Same-sex Relationships, and *Ubuntu*: A Debate in Southern Africa Perspectives

Professor Henry Mbaya
Thokozile J. Mbaya, Ph.D. Student

Ever since John William Colenso (1814-1883), the first Anglican Bishop of Natal, raised the issue of Biblical interpretation in relation to the culture of AmaZulu in the late nineteenth century (Draper 2003), the Anglican Church in Southern Africa has always and continues to wrestle with critical social-cultural and religious issues. Colenso's critical Biblical hermeneutics (Romans and Pentateuch) in light of Zulu culture appeared to challenge the Anglican Church seemingly for not taking African (Zulu) cultural context seriously (Colenso in Draper 2003). Colenso affirmed some aspects of Zulu culture, such as polygamy. Colenso's engagement with Zulu culture underlined his quest for human dignity of the amaZulu.

Colenso's squabbles with Robert Gray in the nineteenth century partly spurred the need to define relationships between the Church of England and colonial churches that also spurred the impulse to the Lambeth Conference of 1867 (Hinchliff 1960, 68, 100). The incident helped to shape Anglican identity considerably.

Two hundred years after that episode, during the past decade, the Anglican Church in Southern Africa faces the issue of human sexuality, an issue that has global dimensions. For Southern African Anglicanism, this issue is particularly unique because of its composition of racial diversity, White people, Africans, colored, Indians, and Whites. In this context, the issue of what it means to be Anglican, and to belong to a sexual minority group, and being human, becomes critical.

This chapter seeks to address the issue of human sexuality in relation to what it means to be Anglican and human in Southern Africa. Is there a relationship between being Anglican, and *Ubuntu,* and in a same-sex relationship, or are these at variance?

Being Anglican, global mission

(Paul Avis 2008,7) states that Anglican identity "started [in England] to be forged in the sixteenth century in the work of (2008, 7) in response to internal political changes and external political threat." Anglican identity was synonymous with English national identity. In the middle and later seventeenth century, Anglicanism went through a renewed identity and "resurgence of theology in response from the threat of the puritans embodied in the commonwealth" (2008, 17).

The Oxford Movement transformed Anglicanism in England, which found its way to South Africa in the nineteenth century (2008, 17).

The history of global Anglicanism under the aegis of British colonialism in the nineteenth century in South Africa entailed God crossing cultural, ethnic, and racial frontiers that culminated in the formation of Anglican Church communities throughout the world. Anglicanism emerged into a global phenomenon expressed in several cultures, spiritualities, racial and ethnic groups. Since then, worldwide Anglicanism has found expression(s) in the regional and local contexts. Hence, global Anglicanism encompasses a diversity of cultural contexts that do impact local contexts. In other words, cultural diversity has become a strong factor of Anglicanism.

Colonial Anglicanism in Southern Africa

Anglican presence in Southern Africa began earnestly with the arrival of Bishop Robert Gray in 1848 (1809-1872). Gray was appointed bishop of Cape Colony in response to the colonial appeals for the Church that lacked administrative and ecclesiastical organization (Hinchliff). Prior to that, the small weak church was governed by the colonial governor on behalf of the Crown. Gray followed Tractarianism (Southey in Suggit and Goedhals 1998, 20–21). Gray also closely associated himself with important High Churchman such as Samuel Wilberforce (1805–1873), Bishop of Oxford.

This Anglicanism came in the shade of Anglo-Catholic spirituality, ethos, and culture. One of the central features of this colonial Anglicanism was domination of male power, thus, as a patriarchal church it excluded women from meaningful participation in leadership structures such as the priesthood (Goedhals 1989, 109). Gender roles were rigidly defined. In its structures and practices, the Anglican Church reflected racism and paternalism that was prevalent in society. Before the current debate on gender and human sexuality, the Anglican in Southern Africa engaged the issue of ordination of women in the 1980s that only passed as a resolution in 1992. It opened "new possibilities of leadership" (Pillay 2017). However, it is the issue of human sexuality (and gender) that emerged in 1990s but has not yet been settled.

Modern global debate on human sexuality

The climax of the Anglican global debate on human sexuality was the Lambeth Conference in 1998, which can be traced to 1978. The Lambeth Resolution 1.10 (1998) on the topic of human sexuality called on each province to reassess its care for and attitude towards persons of homosexual orientation, considering human rights and the need for pastoral concern. This reflects a commitment to treat homosexual individuals with dignity and respect, ensuring their full membership in the Body of Christ while opposing any form of discrimination or homophobia (Anglican Communion 2005).

Furthermore, while the conference upheld heterosexual marriage as the scriptural norm, it recognized the necessity for deep and dispassionate study on the issue of homosexuality, including both scriptural teachings and scientific research. It encouraged dialogue with homosexual individuals and emphasized the need for pastoral care (Anglican Communion 2005).

The conference reiterated that it could not legitimize or bless same-sex unions nor ordain those involved in same-gender unions. However, it underscored the importance of pastoral support and sensitive ministry to all people, regardless of sexual orientation (Anglican Communion 2005). These points here highlight the Anglican Church's efforts to balance adherence to traditional scriptural teachings with a compassionate approach towards individuals with homosexual orientation, promoting dialogue and pastoral care while maintaining doctrinal positions on marriage and sexual conduct.

The resolution did not end the debate. The discussion held, instead, showed an appreciation for the issues raised, but there was no conclusive vote on the matter. This passing over indicated a lack of consensus amongst delegates on the issue of homosexuality as there was a strong belief held to traditional views and teachings on human sexuality, which were reserved between a married man and his wife. The report clearly stated that it was during these discussions in the conference that Resolution 1.10 was amended to state that Scripture, supported by historical tradition, affirmed the traditional teaching upholding faithfulness between a husband and wife in marriage and celibacy for those who are single. The resolution further noted that the Holy Scriptures are clear in teaching that all sexual promiscuity is a sin, including homosexual practices as well as heterosexual relationships outside marriage (Lambeth Resolutions 1988, 10).

This strongly suggested that homosexuality was contrary to the Scriptures in which they believed. The Resolutions (V.1.(d) 1988) further emphasized that the ordained ministers within the Anglican Church communion must lead by example by "repenting" for acting in contradiction with Scripture if or when they knowingly supported such practices. The Lambeth Resolution 1.10 (1998) remains the official teaching on the topic of human sexuality despite it being rejected in some provinces within the Anglican Communion.

Later, in 2008, human sexuality was revisited and debated in Jerusalem, resulting in the GAFCON Jerusalem Declaration, a doctrinal statement formulated by the Global Anglican Future Conference (GAFCON), an international group of conservative Anglican leaders and churches.

The resolution on human sexuality in the GAFCON Jerusalem Declaration reaffirmed traditional Christian teachings on marriage and sexual morality. Specifically, the declaration asserts the following in Declaration number 8:

> We acknowledge God's creation of humankind as male and female and the unchangeable standard of Christian marriage between one man and one woman as the proper place for sexual intimacy and the basis of the family. We repent of our failures to maintain this standard and call for a renewed commitment to lifelong fidelity in marriage and abstinence for those who are not married. (GAFCON 2008).

The declaration affirms that marriage is between one man and one woman, intended by God to be a lifelong union. This is based on the belief that marriage reflects the relationship between Christ and His Church. For this reason, the declaration rejects sexual practices outside of this definition of marriage, including same-sex relationships and any form of sexual activity outside the bounds of heterosexual marriage, which are recognized as sexual immorality. This stance on human sexuality is grounded in the belief that the Bible is the final authority on all matters of faith and conduct, including moral issues. The declaration maintains that any teaching or practice that contradicts the clear teaching of Scripture on sexual ethics is to be rejected, affirming the Lambeth 1998 Conference Resolution 1.10.

By taking this position, the GAFCON Jerusalem Declaration aims to uphold what it considers the orthodox, biblical understanding of human sexuality, and to provide a clear stance in the face of differing views within the wider Anglican Communion. It is seen as a response to what the GAFCON movement views as departures from orthodox biblical teaching by some parts of the Anglican Communion.

The Gene Robinson case in Hampshire

With the emergence of the global human rights culture and open society in the twenty-first century, Anglicanism has found expression in a diversity of cultures, where the issue of human sexuality and gender has come to be at the center. The Anglican communion was thrown into turmoil by two decisions in the early years of the twentieth-first century: the authorizing of public blessings of same-sex relationships by the Diocese of New West Minister in the Anglican Church of Canada and the election, and subsequently confirmation of election, by the General Convention—against the pleas and warnings of the Anglican Primates and the Archbishop of Canterbury—of a priest, living with a partner of the same sex, as Bishop of New Hampshire in the Episcopal Church of the USA (Avis 2007, 76).

The consecration of Bishop V. Gene Robinson, a gay man in a same-sex relationship in 2003, demonstrated changes in the faces of Anglicanism. "Bishop V. Gene Robinson, whose consecration as the first openly gay bishop in the Episcopal Church set off a historic rift in the global Anglican Communion. . ." (Goodstein 2010). The election of Bishop Robinson in the Church shook the Christian world and especially the Episcopal Church (and Anglican Church). It widened the longstanding chasm between theological conservatives and theological liberals in both the Episcopal Church and its parent body, and more so within the Anglican Communion, churches affiliated with the Church of England in more than 160 countries (Goodstein 2010).

The start of the Global Anglican Future Conference (GAfcon) in Jerusalem in 2008 was one among other responses to Robinson's event (Virtue 2024). GAfcon states that it started "when moral compromise, doctrinal error, and the collapse of biblical witness in parts of the Anglican communion had reached such a level that the leaders of the majority of the world's Anglicans felt it was necessary to take a united stand for truth" (Virtue 2024).

On the African continent, since 2003 with a few exceptions, Africa's response to gay clergy and same sex relationships has been very negative. In 2006, led by Peter Akinola, the Church of Nigeria and some African Provinces have stood in opposition to gay clergy and marriage (Polgreen and Goodstein 2006).

In a move attacked by some church leaders as a violation of geographical boundaries, Archbishop Akinola has created an offshoot of his Nigerian church in North America for the discontented Americans. In doing so, he has made himself the kingpin of a remarkable alliance between theological conservatives in North America and the developing world that could tip the power to conservatives in the Anglican Communion, a 77-million member confederation of national churches that trace their roots to the Church of England and the Archbishop of Canterbury (Polgreen and Goodstein 2006).

Tensions on the global stage have found expression in local context(s). Archbishop Thabo expressed the global position on this issue: "the divisions within the Synod of Bishops reflect divisions in the Church as a whole, and we are not at peace with one another on this issue." The Archbishop's concerns suggested serious differences among Anglicans.

The quest for relevance

(Paul Elmen 1988, 336) argues that secularism has shifted theological orientations and imperatives. He observes that we live in a world where, because of the impact of secularism, God is no longer the central reference point; he is opaque. It is a world overshadowed by an aggressive secularist spirit and ethos. In this respect, he argues, there is a need to adapt and orient under the near realities (336). In this respect, he calls for a renewed search for the truth which must be based on "the fullness of experience. . . the search for the truth of the ultimate being which includes the fullness of experience and the wellbeing of the whole created universe" (336).

In his view, in doing theology our point of departure must include international and domestic crises, in view of this study, human sexuality. Then he draws dangers of two extremes. The one is where the "church that preoccupies itself with social reform can easily become the mere agency of social reform." In his view, the alternative is even more scary, . . . "a Church which is comfortable with its role as a cultic enclave, self-righteous and anachronistic, an archaic and dogmatic company, rightly ignored by the world" (336). Then he proposes a solution: "The remedy for such oblivion is surely that commonplace transcendence which was seen by Anglicans from the beginning, and is now widely recognized. We must learn anew to take seriously and then to act upon the claims of our Lord over the total existence universe of his creatures astride our whirling planet."

Anglicanism and Ubuntu spirit and ethos in Southern Africa

To some degree, in the nineteenth century, in his approach to cultural context, specifically on issue of polygamous marriage among the Zulu, Colenso exhibited the liberal spirit as espoused by modern theologians such as Elmen. Colenso's point of departure was Zulu (African context). He affirmed some aspects of the Zulu culture. He appeared to have crossed the boundaries of English cultural chauvinism to an affirmation of some values of the African culture. His openness to African culture earned him the name *Sobantu*, a man/father of the people (Guy 1983, 74).

To the annoyance of some missionaries, Colenso had become the pioneer who affirmed the humanity of the Zulu people. Colenso's liberal approach seems to resonate with some liberal approaches of our time. At the time when polygamy was condemned, Colenso affirmed it in Zulu culture. (Gwilym Colenso 2003, 154) states that, "Unlike the majority of the White settlers and missionaries in Natal and Zululand in the middle of the nineteenth century, Bishop Colenso recognized the inherent value of Zulu custom and belief. He defended polygamy among the Zulu. . ."

Recently in Southern Africa, among others, Thabo Makgoba (in Chapman, Clarke, and Percy, 2015, chapter 26), has taken a liberalist approach in the spirit of Elmen. Makgoba enunciates principles and frameworks in which context and theology can be engaged in Anglican praxis. He asserts that the three Anglican principles, Scripture, tradition, and reason, must be guided by what he calls "holy pragmatism," the core of the incarnation, Word made Flesh (378). From this perspective, he highlights the importance of the incarnation. . . He asserts that the gospel and culture must not be set against each other. He goes on to argue that "God is context neutral" and that his truth has always been revealed to us in and through culture, even as it critiques culture and calls for its redemption (379). He clinches his argument by citing his predecessor, Njongonkulu Ndungane.

Sometimes we speak of the need to "baptize culture." This is no cursory wipe with a damp cloth to produce a religious veneer. Baptism is the radical transformation that comes through with burial through Christ and being raised with him—every culture must die to the priorities, the loyalties, the idols of this world, and find new, authentic, life-giving, contemporary expression, transfigured under the lordship of Jesus, Saviour and Redeemer (378-379).

Magoba's perspectives are crucial for reflecting on the issue of same-sex relationships and Ubuntu in Southern Africa. There are multiple definitions of Ubuntu.

Scholars Jacob (Mugumbate and Andrew Nyaguru 2013, 82) describe Ubuntu as "an African philosophy that emphasizes being human through other people." The concept is understood by seeing individuals as having relations and being connected to others. Ramathate Dolamo (2013, 1) explained this concept by stating that Ubuntu is "an integral part of African ethics steeped in issues of liberation, development, identity, etc. It has to do with a person's integrity and dignity." It denotes an African form of humanism, which has been broadly expressed in the phrase "I am because we are; since we are, therefore I am"—*umuntu ngumuntu ngabantu* in isiZulu (Mbiti 1969, 108).

However, they all affirm the individual and the recognition of the other person's being. Tutu's definition of Ubuntu is "we believe that a person is a person through other persons, that humanity is caught up, bound up, inextricably with yours. When I dehumanize you, I inexorably dehumanize myself" (Tutu 1999).

Ubuntu recognizes the humanity of all as created in the image of God, thus making the imago Dei the essence of humanity's identity. The *imago Dei* foundation of *Ubuntu* determines humanity and denies anyone or any institution the right to decide the superiority or inferiority of the other. Molly Manyonganise holds that, as originally developed, *Ubuntu* theology is not gender inclusive. As an ideology that is gaining wide African acceptability, scholars like Manyonganise have expressed concern at the lack of gender inclusivity in the discourse of Ubuntu, especially in the patriarchal societies of Africa where the male determines the identity of a person.

In Southern Africa, the advent and unfolding of colonialism were accompanied by cultural violence, in which Anglicanism played a crucial role. In its mission, the Anglican Church entailed the crossing of African cultural values. One of these entailed the African cultural values of human Africanness—respecting and caring for others. Defined as human charity, tolerance, and acceptance, Ubuntu is about feeling for others and hospitality. It is about welcoming the other in spite of differences.

An exception to this attitude, in responding to the dynamism of Zulu cultures, Colenso, inspired by liberal theology of FD Maurice, to some degree, was more accommodating to Zulu culture (see Maclean, 2003). Under the influence of Magema Fuze, Colenso was critical to his English cultural assumptions of superiority. He had a positive attitude toward some Zulu cultural beliefs, which he considered as not in conflict with Biblical traditions and cultures. However, colonial Anglicanism, just as in African cultures in Southern Africa, were patriarchal and sexist.

Concerning addressing human rights and gay and lesbian persons, Adriaan van Klinken (2020) has identified the role of two notable Anglican leaders who famously called on Ubuntu within the Anglican Church. He stated that "…Archbishop

Njongonkulu Ndungane [and Archbishop Tutu] have been supportive of the idea to acknowledge and safeguard the human rights of gay and lesbian people in the new South Africa" (van Klinken 2020). Van Klinken further states that, "Tutu himself has explicitly and repeatedly related the struggle for sexual freedom to the earlier anti-apartheid struggle for racial liberation." As he famously put it, "If the church, after the victory over apartheid, is looking for a worthy moral crusade, then this is it: the fight against homophobia and heterosexism. I pray that we will engage in it with the same dedication and fervor which we showed against the injustice of racism, so that we may rehabilitate the gospel of Jesus Christ" (van Klinken 2020).

Human sexuality debate in ACSA

The debate on human sexuality in the Anglican Church of Southern Africa (ACSA) emerged very late. In the Provincial Synod that sat in 2016, "Anglican bishops from across Southern Africa resolved. . .that gay and lesbian partners who enter same-sex civil unions under South African law should be welcomed into congregations as full members of the church. However, bishops were at that time divided over whether to marry same-sex couples in church (TIMESLIVE 2023)."

Then "the Archbishop set up an 'Archbishop's Commission on Human Sexuality' in response to the 2016 Synod debate. . ."(TIMESLIVE 2023). It was this body which brought. . .[in 2023] Synod the proposal for a highly circumscribed experiment which would have allowed blessings for same-sex unions on a basis similar to that adopted when the Province first allowed the ordination of women in 1992" (TIMESLIVE 2023).

At the Provincial Synod of 2016, the ACSA produced a statement which affirmed same-sex relationships as follows. In his letter *To the Laos, The People of God*, (Archbishop Thabo 2016) wrote:

> We reaffirm our assurance to them that they are loved by God and that all baptized, believing and faithful persons, regardless of sexual orientation, are full members of the Body of Christ. Many of these are baptized and confirmed members of the Church and are seeking the pastoral care, moral direction of the Church, and God's transforming power for the living of their lives and the ordering of relationships.

The significance of the statement lies in the fact that it affirms the interrelationship between same sexual orientation, the loving and care of God, and belonging to the Body of Christ. It similarly significant that Makgoba affirmed the pastoral responsibilities of the church in relation to people of same sexual orientation. In another section, the bishops further asserted that, "We are of one mind that gay, lesbian, and transgendered members of our church share in full membership as baptized members of the Body of Christ. . ." (Archbishop Thabo 2016).

The bishops expounded on the implications of this resolution, namely, that no person whether adult or minor must be discriminated on the grounds of sexual orientation. "No child brought for baptism should be refused merely because of the sexual orientation of the parents, and particular care should be taken against stigmatising not only parents but their children too" (Archbishop Thabo 2016). Addressing same sex marriage was not enough without seeking to address the issue of stigma. A statement was not enough, but more importantly it provided for mechanisms and systems to be put in place which could guide the process. Makgoba went on to assert that:

> We also tried at the Synod of Bishops to draw up guidelines for clergy wanting to bless couples in same-sex unions, or who want to enter same-sex unions themselves. We constituted a group of bishops reflecting a cross-section of our views to discuss such guidelines. On this issue, I had to report back to the Synod, the only agreement we reached is that we were not of one mind (Archbishop Thabo 2016).

Division amongst bishops reveal the controversial nature of the issue compounded by the diversities of their cultural contexts. He went to state that:

> Our differences do not only revolve around the theology of marriage, but are also a result of different pastoral realities in different dioceses. For example, most of our dioceses across Southern Africa are predominantly rural, and for many the urgent priorities of food security, shelter, healthcare and education crowd out debate on the issue

of human sexuality. In some rural dioceses, responding to challenges to the Church's restrictions on polygamous marriages is a much higher pastoral priority (Archbishop Thabo 2016).

It is strange that the letter seems to suggest that the issue was not priority number one to the rural-based dioceses of the Province, in light of the fact that it threatened the split of the global Anglican communion. The statement seems to suggest that for the rural-based dioceses this issue was of a less priority for them as it was for urban dioceses. He went on to assert that:

> As a consequence, the Synod of Bishops has agreed that we will continue to regard ourselves bound by the broad consensus in the Anglican Communion, expressed by the Lambeth Conference in 1998, which is that we "cannot advise the legitimising or blessing of same-sex unions nor ordaining those involved in same gender unions." Having said that, we did address the questions of whether that decision is immutable, whether it has replaced scripture, and when a Province of the Communion, or a diocese within a Province may deviate from it (Archbishop Thabo 2016).

In this respect, the Lambeth Conference 1998 resolution affected the status of Tutu van Furth. The resolution made her marriage illegitimate, and by extension her license as a priest revocable. The bishop's critical reflection on the resolution was not helpful, either, as the resolution did not offer room for engagement.

Drawing on the country's history of racial division and polarization was very significant as it made the bishops view Christian charity as crucial in maintaining harmony in the body of Christ, but at the same time it was a weakness as it seemed to hinder them from having a courageous conversation. This historical foundation could have emboldened them to engage with the issue with the seriousness it deserved. It is similarly significant that the bishops asserted that the issue did not cause divisions among them—to the extent of disavowing each other as brothers and sisters in Christ. Archbishop Thabo finally concluded,

> Given that we share such broad and deep foundations of faith, when, as Bishops in Synod, we consider questions of human sexuality, we feel sharp pain and great distress at our own differences and at the breaches and divisions within the wider Anglican Communion. Yet we strongly affirm that we are united in this: that none of us feels called to turn to another and say "I no longer consider you a Christian, a brother in Christ, a member of the body of Christ." None of us says "I am no longer in communion with you." We find that our differing views on human sexuality take second place alongside the strength of our overpowering conviction of Christ among us. As long as we, the Bishops of this Province, know unity in Christ in this way, human sexuality is not, and cannot be allowed to be, for us a church-dividing issue (Archbishop Thabo 2016).

Makgoba's statement reflected the atmosphere in the Anglican Communion then, especially the Global South's, and especially West and East Africans were responding to the developments in the USA and Canada.

The debate on human sexuality within the Anglican Church of Southern Africa led to the Provincial Synod Resolutions in 2017. The Provincial Synod held in 2017 prioritized human sexuality in its agenda, Resolution 9. The Synod discussed the magnitude of the awareness of human sexuality in different spheres of society, including within the Anglican Church. The Synod resolved:

- to acknowledge that the Archbishop has constituted a Provincial Commission on Human Sexuality.
- Make it clear that the dioceses remain committed to achieving a full and inclusive ministry for all people, including those from the LGBTQI community.
- Develop further guidelines for pastoral ministry in consultation with the ACSA and those identified as members of the LGBTQI community.
- Set up a workgroup that will help create deeper commitments to networking across boundaries and intentionally working at the grassroots level to address current issues related to human sexuality.
- Encourage the diocese to support the implementation of such guidelines that allow us to minister fully to all people, including the LGBTQI community (ACTS and Resolutions Booklet of Synod 2017, 50)

These Provincial Synod resolutions on human sexuality reflect a commitment to ongoing dialogue, pastoral care, and sensitivity while upholding the Church's traditional teachings on marriage and sexuality. The Church recognizes the diversity of views within its community and seeks to navigate these differences with respect and a spirit of discernment. The 2017 resolutions emphasized the need for sensitivity and pastoral care, recognising the diversity of views within the Church. However, they did not approve the blessing of same-sex unions or marriages, instead calling for continued discussion and discernment. More recently, in 2023, ACSA failed to agree on blessing same-sex couples. (TIMESLIVE 2023) reported that:

> Anglican bishops in Southern Africa have failed to reach consensus on blessing same-sex unions during church services, ruling out church marriages for same-sex couples. Archbishop Thabo Makgoba of Cape Town on Monday said, "the divisions within the Synod of Bishops reflect the divisions in the Church as a whole, and we are not at peace with one another on this issue." However, the bishops have resolved to craft special prayers suitable for providing pastoral care to couples in same-sex civil unions.
>
> Following the constitution of the Provincial Commission on Human Sexuality by the Archbishop of Cape Town in 2017, in December 2017, the diocese of False Bay (Bishop Margaret Virtue) (to which the authors belong), constituted the Working Group of three members which essentially endorsed the Provincial

Commission and its aims… "Ensure that the Diocese of False Bay, by majority, supports the implementation of Guidelines that allow us to minister fully to all God's people, including the LGBTI community." (Letter, Bishop Margaret Vertue, 18/12/2917).

To summarize, efforts toward the blessing of same-sex couples continue to merely endorse a committment to a full and inclusive ministry to all people, including those of the LGBTI community. There are even those who work intentionally on a grassroots level to vigorously address the current and rising issues related to human sexuality. And yet, the denial of same-sex blessings still remains.

The case of Mpho Tutu van Furth

The Anglican Church's attitude to Mpho Tutu van Furth's married status to Van Furth seems to be at variance with the Anglicanism ethos of inclusion and the spirit of *Ubuntu*. It seems to demonstrate the tension between what it means to be Anglican and being gay. Mpho Tutu van Furth is Desmond Tutu's youngest child. In her early 30s, while running various church outreach projects in Worcester, Massachusetts, Tutu van Furth realized that she had a call to the ordained ministry (Cornell 2022). In 2003, in her 40s, she was ordained in the Episcopal Church of the United States.

The same year, it elected its first openly gay bishop, sending shockwaves through the Anglican Communion (Cornell 2022). Mpho Tutu van Furth married her same-sex partner, Marceline van Furth, in 2015. Following this, she resigned her ministerial license within the ACSA because the Church's current position did not allow for clergy in same-sex marriages to retain their licenses (Cornell 2022). The ACSA, in response, stated that their canons and policies did not permit clergy in same-sex marriages to hold a license to minister (Cornwell, 2022). This stance led to Tutu van Furth's resignation from her clerical duties within the Church.

The withdrawal of Tutu's ministerial license based on her gay marriage and sexuality, despite the Anglican Church of Southern Africa (ACSA) officially, on paper, leaving room for acceptance of same-sex marriages, is at variance with the spirit of *ubuntu*. The concept of *ubuntu* underlines the ACSA's approach to pastoral care, advocating for the dignity and worth of every individual, regardless of their sexuality. While the Church maintains its doctrinal stance on marriage, it also seeks to embody the principles of Ubuntu by providing care and support to all members.

Anna Nolte and Charlene Downing (2019, 11) assert that "respect and dignity are considered the building blocks in the culture of Ubuntu..." Further, they assert that these values "... lead to an acknowledgment of the rights and responsibilities of every citizen." (11) They conclude, stating that, "Any other person should be treated with respect..." (11) In addition, the needs of others are viewed to be equal to the needs of the individual. And thus, no individual is more sacred than another.

"The respect of another's humanity is absolute..." (11). It would appear as if Tutu van Furth was treated with less dignity when Bishop Hess went to take her ministerial license. She stated, "I'm not spoiling for a fight; it has to be a conversation. But the gift of being in a country where same-sex marriage is legal should mean the church can be the place where we can have a theological conversation about the nature of marriage."

Among other issues, TEAC Anglican Way Consultation (2007) has identified "negative aspects of colonial heritage, self-serving abuse of power and privilege" as critical issues that undervalue the contribution of women. In Southern Africa, one of these is patriarchy and paternalism. South Africa has inherited colonial and apartheid disvalues of male domination of women. Women are seen as "children." In spite of some progress made, the Anglican Church still reflects some of these in its structure and in its attitudes. The church's attitude toward Tutu van Furth seems to suggest the treatment of a minor.

The ACSA faces the challenge of balancing its doctrinal teachings with the principles of Ubuntu, striving to respect and honor the dignity of individuals while upholding traditional views on marriage and sexuality. The case of Mpho Tutu van Furth highlights the complexities and challenges faced by the Church in addressing issues related to human sexuality within its community. State Law provides for same sex marriages, while the Church does not provide for it in its laws.

Tutu van Furth says "deep-searching discussions and debates" will continue (Cornwell 2022). "Those who are vehemently opposed to same-sex marriage really dug in their heels (2022)" in response to her marriage, "and those who have been letting the issue slide, so to speak, have realized that they can't afford to let it slide for another umpteen years, umpteen synods. And that we really do have to talk about marriage and same-sex unions, and that we do have to address all of our membership and not just those with whom we find easy agreement" (2022).

"Nevertheless, as Anglicans we are keenly aware that our common life and engagement in God's mission are tainted with shortcomings and failure. . ." (2022). One of these in Southern Africa is patriarchal attitudes and practices. Men regard themselves as superior to women and cannot countenance females who seem to assume "traditional" male roles. (Southern) Africa has been the domain of male power where women are socialized into subordinate roles. In southern Africa, patriarchy as a cultural challenge seem to be buttressed by ecclesiastical patriarchy.

Barbara Nussbaum (2003, 3), asserts that, "Because of its emphasis on our common humanity and the ethical call to embody our communal responsiveness in the world, *ubuntu* offers an alternative way to re-create a world that works for all. . . how to live together with respect, compassion and dignity and justice and to re-organize resources accordingly." In this respect, the issue of marriage of Tutu van Furth and her partner is an issue of justice, dignity, and compassion.

Tutu van Furth deserves to be treated with justice. From the Ubuntu point of view, denial of their sexuality and marriage violates the spirit and principles of Ubuntu, their humanness. It contravenes the spirit of communality, compassion, and respect. By the same token, it is in variance with the Anglican ethos of unity in diversity. Anglicanism is about accommodating the other—recognizing that diversity and difference is not a weakness but a strength.

Conclusion

This chapter set out to discuss the issue of same-sex relationships in relation to ubuntu and Anglicanism in Southern Africa. As a background to the context in Southern Africa, the chapter first highlighted the history of global Anglicanism as a prelude to the center of debate on the issue of same-sex relationship in Southern African Anglicanism. In particular, it has traced the same-sex debate within global Anglicanism when in emerged in 2000s, the context and event that culminated in the election of American Gene Robinson, a bishop in a same-sex partnership in Hampshire 2003. From this spectrum, using Ubuntu, and in dialogue with Anglicanism, the paper critiqued the manner in which Tutu van Furth, married to van Furth, was handled by the church. It has argued that the church's treatment of Tutu van Furth seems to be at variance not only with the comprehensive nature of Anglicanism, its ethos and spirit, but also in contradiction to the Ubuntu spirit of humanness.

References

ACNA, "SA bishops: Same-sex couples "full members" of church; no-change on marriage

https://www.anglicannews.org/news/2016/02/sa-bishops-same-sex -couples-full-members-of-church-no-change-on-marriage.aspx.

Avis, Paul., *Anglicanism and the Christian Church: Theological Resources in Historical Perspective* (Edinburgh: T & T Clark, 2002).

Alvis, P., *The Identity of Anglicanism: Essentials of Anglican Ecclesiology* (London, New York: Bloomsbury, 2008).

Anglican Communion, *The Lambeth Conference Resolutions Archive from 1998*, 2005.

Anglican Consultative Council. Accessed from: https://www.anglican communion.org/resources/document-library.aspx?author=Lambeth +Conference&year=1998.

Colenso, G. 2003. "The Pentateuch in Perspective: Bishop Colenso's Biblical Criticism in its Colonial Context" In *The Eye of the Storm*, *edited by* J.A. Draper (Pietermaritzburg, Cluster Publications), 136–168.

Cornwell, M., "Interview: Mpho Tutu van Furth: Apartheid, my famous father and gay marriage." *Premier Christianity Magazine*. https://www.premierchristianity.com/interviews/mpho-tutu-van -furth-apartheid-my-famous-father-and-gay-marriage/13367 .article.

Dolamo, R., "Botho/Ubuntu: the heart of African ethics." *Scriptura*: *Journal for Contextual Hermeneutics in Southern Africa*, 112(1): 1–10.

Draper, J., *The Eye of the Storm* (Pietermaritzburg: Cluster Publications, 2003).

Emen, P., "Anglican Morality," in *The Study of Anglicanism, edited by* S. Sykes and J. Booty (London: SPCK, 1988), 325–338.

GAFCON Global Anglicans, The Jerusalem Declaration, 29th June 2008. The Global Anglican Future Conference (GAFCON). Accessed from: https://www.gafcon.org/resources /the-jerusalem-declaration.

Goedhals, M., "From Paternalism to Partnership?" In *In Bounty in bondage: the Anglican Church in Southern Africa: essays in honor of Edward King, Dean of Cape Town*, edited by Frank England and Torquil Paterson (Cape Town: Ravan Press), 104–129.

Goodstein, L., "First Openly Gay Bishop to Retire." *New York Times*, 2010. https://www.nytimes.com/2010/11/07/us/07bishop.html.

Guy, J., *The Heretic: A Study of the Life of John William Colenso* (Johannesburg: Ravan Press, 1983).

Hinchliff, P., "The History of the Anglican Church in South Africa with special reference to the development of constitution and organization." B.D. thesis: Univ. of Oxford. In Southey, *Change and Challenge. Essays Commemorating the 150th Anniversary of the Arrival of Robert Gray as First Bishop of Cape Town (20th February 1848)*, 1963.

Hinchliff, P., "The theory and practice of Prayer Book revision in South Africa," *The Journal of Ecclesiastical History* 11.1 (1960):87–97.

Maclean, I. S., "The Twin Pillars of Heathenism: American Missionaries, Bishop Colenso and Converts in Conflict— Polygamy and Ukulobola in Nineteenth-Century Natal and Zululand, South Africa" In *The Eye of the Storm*, edited by Jonathan Draper (Pietermaritzburg: Cluster Publications), 256-265.

Makgoba, T. C., "Politics" In *The Oxford Handbook of Anglican Studies*, edited by M Chapman and S. Clarke (Oxford: Oxford University Press, 2015), 372–383.

Manyonganise, M., "Oppressive and liberative: A Zimbabwean woman's reflections on Ubuntu." *Verbum et Ecclesia* 36(2): 1-7. Retrieved from http://dx.doi.org/10.4102/ve.v36i2.1438.

Mbiti, J. S., *African Religions and Philosophy* (Nairobi: East African Educational Publishers Ltd., 1969).

Mugumbate, J. and Nyanguru, A., "Exploring African philosophy: The value of Ubuntu in social work." *African Journal of Social Work*, 3 (1), 82-100.

Nolte, A. and Downing, C., "Ubuntu: The Essence of Being and Caring A Concept Analysis." *HOLISTIC NURSING PRACTICE*, January/February 2019;33(1):9–16. https://journals.lww.com/hnpjournal/abstract/2019/01000/ubuntu_the_essence_of_caring_and_being__a_concept.3.aspx.

Nussbaum, B., "Ubuntu: Reflections of a South African on Our Common Humanity." *World Business Academy*. Volume 17, Issue 1, February 12, 2003. https://www.researchgate.net/publication/237672969.

Polgreen, L. and Goodstein, L. "At Axis of Episcopal Split, an Anti-Gay Nigerian." *The New York Times*, Dec. 25, 2006. https://www.nytimes.com/2006/12/25/world/africa/at-axis-of-episcopal-split-an-antigay-nigerian.html.

Pillay, M., "Women, Priests and the Anglican Church in Southern Africa: Reformation of Holy Hierarchies." *Consensus*. Volume 38 Issue 1, *Reformation: Then, Now, and Onward. Varied Voices, Insightful Interpretations*.

Tutu, D., *No future without forgiveness* (NY: Doubleday, 1999).

Van Klinken, A., "Desmond Tutu's Long History of Fighting For Lesbian and Gay Rights," *The Conversation*. https://theconversation.com/desmond-tutus-long-history-of-fighting-for-lesbian-and-gay-rights-131598, 2020.

Virtue, D., "GAFCON and GFSA: A Delicate Dance." https://virtueonline.org/gafcon-and-gsfa-delicate-dance, 2024.

CHAPTER SIX

Saved by a *Black Christ*, Thanks to Father Tutu

Wilhelm Verwoerd[1]

M y first encounter with Ronald Harrison's profoundly unsettling painting, *Black Christ*[2], was in an Anglican cathedral nearly thirty years ago. I was working as a researcher in the Truth and Reconciliation Commission (TRC) office in Cape Town and regularly attended services in the nearby St George's Cathedral. After a special reconciliation service, on 16 November 1997, my attention was drawn to a big painting in one corner of the cathedral. It was indeed unusual to see the Christ figure depicted as a Black person—rather than the typical Western portrayal of a "Whitey in a nightie' (Harrison 2008, 26). I recognized the face of Chief Albert Luthuli, former president of the ANC (Luthuli 2006). But my eyes were drawn to a figure in the bottom left corner: a White soldier with a long spear piercing the side of the Black figure on the cross. This Roman centurion had a disturbingly familiar face. Pictures, paintings, statutes of a revered Prime Minister

1. Senior Researcher and facilitator, Centre for the Study of the Afterlife of Violence and the Reparative Quest (AVReQ), Stellenbosch University, South Africa (https://avreq.sun.ac.za/).

2. Ronald Harrison, *Black Christ*, 1962, acrylic on canvas. (https://javettup .art/artworks/black-christ)

Verwoerd featured prominently in my Afrikaner Nationalist upbringing. But we were not only members of the same "White tribe," the Afrikaners, we belonged to the same church, the Dutch Reformed Church (DRC). And Dr H. F. Verwoerd is *Oupa* Hendrik, my grandfather.

Figure 2: "Grandpa and Grandma Verwoerd with their grandchildren, Pretoria, 8 September 1964

In this picture, taken on the porch of the Prime Minister's official residence, Libertas, I happen to be the 6 months-old baby on *Oupa* Hendrik's lap. From this time to the time I encountered the *Black Christ* in 1997, I had already undergone a major political and religious transformation away from my earlier enthusiastic membership of the DRC and proud membership of the Verwoerd family (Verwoerd 1997). Still, the image of Verwoerd as the person piercing the side of Luthuli was deeply upsetting.

Almost 40 years later, in so-called "post-apartheid" South Africa, I continue with the struggle to fully place myself within the painful history conveyed by *Black Christ*. My embodied faith journey has become a descending spiral staircase of returning again and again to this question: how can I look honestly, open-heartedly at *both* these images—the emotionless soldier and the smiling, caring grandfather; how do I face the prophetic truth of an "iconic painting of the struggle for liberation" (Martin in Harrison 2008, xiv) *and* accept the intimate intergenerational connections symbolized by *Oupa*'s smile and the unexpected milk bottle in his almost motherly hand? (Verwoerd 1997, 2001, 2019, 2021, 2022).

In this chapter, I continue my quest with this question. Through a reflection on a "pastoral tea" conversation with Archbishop Tutu, I highlight how his radically inclusive ubuntu has midwifed my rebirth, as a White Afrikaner Verwoerd with a transformed, embodied commitment to follow Christ in post-1994 South Africa. I express more deeply my gratitude to "South Africa's confessor" (Battle 2021), amongst others[3], for enabling me to accept *Black Christ* as a painful, deeply liberating invitation to participate in the mystery of the

---

3. Space does not allow me to include the vital role of Pumla Gobodo-Madikizela, another Black Anglican South African, a former TRC commissioner, founding director of AVReQ and winner of the 2024 Templeton Prize (Verwoerd 2018, 2019).

Incarnation. I then continue the conversation with Father Tutu by revisiting his warning to not take on a "burden that is unbearable." I draw on my current racial repair practice and Boulding's helpful notion of the "200-year present"—a generational sense of self and time that includes both my grandfather and the fact that I recently became a grandfather myself. The next step is a cautious interpretation of *Black Christ*—specifically, the radiant gaze of the Luthuli figure— as a symbol of hope, even for descendants of the tormenting centurion and his henchman. In this search for embodied hope in *Black Christ,* I find inspiration in Tutu's spirituality. I also draw on the contemplative, "apophatic"[4] roots of my faith, in which the Centre for Christian Spirituality, founded by Tutu in 1986, played a vital role. But first it is important to give a bit more detail on the birth and theology of *Black Christ.*

Birth and reception of *Black Christ*

One evening in late December 1961, a 21-year-old Ron Harrison was lying in bed. Haunted by recent political events such as the Sharpeville massacre, the arrest of ANC, PAC, and SACP political leaders, more and more apartheid legislation and "the government's antipathy towards Chief Luthuli," he had become "obsessed with the idea of taking some constructive action in the

---

4. Etymologically, "apophatic" comes from the combination of "phasis" (speech) with the preposition "apo" (away from) and in theology is linked to "negative," non-affirmative speech about God vs. the "kataphatic" "positive" naming of God (Williams 2019, xvii-xviii).

liberation movement" using his artistic talent. That evening "a thought flashed through" his head: "How could a government that professed to be Christian perpetrate such immoral deeds and inflict so much pain and suffering on its own countrymen simply because [they] were of another race, another color, another creed? Verwoerd and [Minister of Justice] Vorster were wreaking havoc in their quest for White supremacy and Afrikaner domination, and in the process the Black races— in fact all races that were not classified 'White'—were being crucified."[5]

In his autobiography, Harrison relates how his own family was destroyed by his father opting to be classified "White," leaving his "colored" wife and children. He also describes the "birth of *Black Christ*":

> The picture of a suffering Christ at the scene of His crucifixion surged through my mind, but the vision forming in my mind's eye was rather unusual in that the figure on the cross was a Black man! I realized that I could depict the suffering of the Black people and equate this with the suffering of Christ.
>
> After many rough sketches, I finally settled on the facial features of my Christ figure. Who better than Chief Albert Luthuli, who had just been awarded the Nobel Peace Prize. . .Luthuli was a revered icon of the struggle against oppression. . . I decided that the

---

5. For more historical background, see Davenport (1986), Kenney (1980), Biko (2012).

architects of apartheid also had to be brought into the scene. I had it! Verwoerd and Vorster would be portrayed as two Roman centurions, the tormentors of Christ. Verwoerd would be piercing the side of Christ, and his henchman, Vorster, would be standing with the sponge of vinegar and gall. A colored Madonna and an Asian St John would complete the scene (Harrison, 2008, 25-26).

Harrison expected the painting to be controversial. Though widely welcomed in anti-apartheid church circles, the White DRC mouthpiece, *Die Kerkbode*, condemned it as blasphemous and the major Afrikaner newspaper *Die Burger* called for its banning. Following an official complaint from the DRC, the Censorship Board declared *Black Christ* "unfit for public exhibition" because it "gave offence to the religious convictions and feelings of a section of the population."

By then, the provocative protest artwork was smuggled out to the UK where it was used to raise awareness and funds for the anti-apartheid struggle. Harrison was repeatedly and brutally interrogated and tortured to reveal the whereabouts of his painting, leaving permanent damage to his health. The painting was eventually returned to South Africa in 1997, temporarily displayed in St George's Cathedral, before given a permanent home in the Iziko Museum in Cape Town (Harrison 2008; De Gruchy 2001, 230-232).

Theology of *Black Christ*

Ron Harrison's courageous visual comparison between the apartheid era suppression of "non-Whites" and the crucifixion of Jesus enabled his prophetic critique to transcend political and moral denunciation, to bring perhaps the deepest wounding of those represented by the Luthuli figure to the surface. As Tutu put it in his Preface to Steve Biko's classic *I Write What I like* (Biko 2012, ix): "[T]he most awful aspect of oppression and injustice was not the untold suffering it visited on its victims and survivors. . . No, it was the fact that apartheid could. . .actually make many of them doubt whether they were indeed God's children. That I have described as almost the ultimate blasphemy."[6]

The tragic irony is that the DRC's rejection of *Black Christ* as "blasphemous" betrayed also their revered John Calvin's theology of social justice. Wolterstorff stresses that for Calvin, claims of love and justice towards other human beings are grounded in the *inalienable* iconicity of *all* human beings as being created "in the image of God." Therefore, "to treat unjustly one of these human earthlings in whom God delights is to bring sorrow to God. To wound his beloved is to wound him" (Wolterstorff, 1987:20). Calvin's discussion of the Eucharist brings Christ explicitly into this radical picture: "We shall benefit very much from the Sacrament if this thought is

---

6. See also the reference to Biko as a Christlike "icon" in Lentz and Gateley, *Christ in the Margins*, quoted in De Gruchy 2008:140—"those who serve the poor, struggle for justice and peace, and live lives of compassion, also reflect who Christ is for us, today."

impressed and engraved on our minds that none of the brethren can be injured, despised, rejected, abused or in any way offended by us without at the same time injuring, despising and abusing Christ by the wrongs we do" (Institutes, IV 8:38, quoted in Wolterstorff 1987:20).

I am aware that the glaring gap between this aspect of Calvin's theology and the reality of Calvinism within my mother church is not restricted to White Afrikaners within the DRC. The prophetic truth of *Black Christ* sadly transcends the context that gave rise to its birth: "As a result of centuries of crusades and wars, pogroms, the Holocaust, racism and oppression, justified by Christians as the will of God and pursued under the banner of the cross, Christians have crucified Jesus afresh" (De Gruchy 2006:134). The racialized crucifixion scene of *Black Christ*, however, draws specific attention to the widespread tendency amongst historically privileged White Christians to separate the cross of Jesus from ongoing crucifixions in history. The *Black Christ* confronts someone like me with the profound challenge of responding to Black theologians' call for an incarnational religious imagination that relates "the message of the cross to one's own social reality, to see that they [we] are crucifying again the Son of God" (Heb 6:6) (Cone 2017,158; Williams 2014; Mofokeng 1983).

In this regard, I find Cone's explicit connection between the message of the cross and the "lynching tree" particularly relevant. This connection includes his critique of mainstream White theology: "It takes a lot of theological blindness. . .[to write] thousands of books about Jesus' cross without remarking on the analogy between the crucifixion of Jesus and the lynching of Black people. . . especially since the vigilantes were White Christians who claimed to worship the Jew lynched in Jerusalem" (2017, 159). I resonate with his further statement that "the lynching tree frees the cross from the false pieties of well-meaning Christians;" the cross "needs the lynching tree to remind Americans of the reality of suffering—to keep the cross from becoming a symbol of abstract, sentimental piety" (2017, 161). On the other hand, he reminds us that "the lynching tree also needs the cross, without which it simply becomes an abomination. It is the cross that points in the direction of hope, the confidence that there is a dimension to life beyond the reach of the oppressor" (2017, 161–2).

In similar vein, the cross clearly needs a *Black Christ*. This religious icon confronts someone like me with a painful truth: what Verwoerd and his fervent supporters did to Luthuli and his people, we also did to Christ (Mt 25:38-40, Ac 9:4-5). Even though I was *sincere* in my pious, Dutch Reformed, "Afrikaner Calvinist" (De Gruchy 1991) following of (a White) Jesus, I thus remain complicit in the deepest wounding of fellow human beings and, therefore, the re-crucifixion of Christ.[7] A crucifixion that continues through the haunting of post-1994 South Africa by the "afterlife of apartheid" (Gobodo-Madikizela 2023; 2016).

---

7. I stand on the shoulders of many earlier critics of the DRC, such as Beyers Naudé (Hansen 2005), Boesak (1984), Kritzinger (2008), and I am indebted to a younger generation of prophetic scholars, for example Van Wyngaard (2014, 2019). On the wider historical complicity of White South African Christianity, see Kleinschmidt (1972, ed.); *TRC Report*, Vol. 4.

But the *Black Christ*, for pre- and post-1994 South Africa, also needs the cross, as a paradoxical symbol of hope. I need the cross, as a descendant of the centurion-with-a-spear, as a co-crucifier, to have "confidence that there is a dimension to life beyond the reach of the oppressor." However, over decades of grappling with *Black Christ*, often feeling overwhelmed and wanting to run away, I have learnt that I cannot cultivate this incarnational imagination on my own, I cannot remain faithful to this radical Christian discipleship by myself. Along this way Archbishop Tutu became a key spiritual guide.

A liberating pastoral tea with Father Tutu

A highlight of my time in the TRC was to see the "the Arch" in action as chairperson and to have a few serious conversations with him. Twenty years later, during a follow-up to the Faith Communities hearing of the TRC in 2016 (Thesnaar & Hansen 2020), we meet briefly during a tea break. He unexpectedly invites me to continue our exchange about ancestors and reconciliation at a later stage. Despite his fragile health, he makes time, on 10 August 2016, for a pastoral cup of tea. In preparation for the rest of this chapter I include the full conversation here.

Sitting in a large comfortable chair he apologizes, in Afrikaans, for not standing up to greet me. He invites me to come and sit next to him, says a short prayer and asks, "How are you?" I'm very aware of how little time we have so I jump in at the deep end:

I am well, thanks, Father, though I am spending a lot of time with a troublesome ancestor lately. . .and with the Black Christ painting. I've come to the conclusion that I CANNOT reconcile that painting with the picture I sent you of myself as a baby on my grandfather's knee— the worlds are so far apart. But I see it as part of my commitment to reconciliation to face the pain that is represented in that painting, without demonizing my grandfather. To look for ways how I can help to transform that pain, from a spiritual depth, not just at a political level, and that's why I thought your wisdom would be very precious.

He responds in a soft voice, "I think already the very fact of you being concerned about the anguish and the pain that was caused by a policy. . ." Then he interrupts himself and confirms the length of that Soldier's Spear:

A policy which he didn't start, remember! He came in a long line of premiers. But he was a very, very clever man. He could argue the hind leg off a horse. One obviously wishes that he had been on the right side. Having said ALL of that, he was a human being like all of us, subject to the same pressures. At that time his White compatriots clearly wanted a separation between the races, that they should have a superior, advantaged position. I suppose he would have been silly—having gotten into power by those people—to do a somersault.

In typical generous fashion he continues:

> I think that we should not demonize them, whilst not
> exculpating them. They were under the pressures of their
> time: they had just come out of a bruising war; they had
> sought to escape from the British, to find a place where
> they could live as they wanted to live. . .all of those things
> left their mark. And succeeding generations exhibited,
> 'We are a minority surrounded by very hostile barbarians;
> if we want to retain our racial purity we have to separate
> ourselves from them. And if we want to maintain our
> hegemony, then you have to keep them down.'

He gives another Tutu laugh. I shake my head at how these
people, "my people," dared to call ourselves "Christians," despite
the glaring gulf between vision and practice. He reminds me of
how many people today are still caught up in racial stereotypes
before returning to my controversial ancestor.

> I myself would say that you have to be generous in your
> judgment of him. He was not a vicious man, who just
> wanted to be cruel for the sake of being cruel. He truly
> believed that it was possible to have races existing side by
> side, but separately—separate schools, separate churches,
> and not mingling socially. I am not trying to whitewash
> him, I am just saying. . .

He challenges me, three times, to accept this particular
ancestor: "In any case, there is not very much you can do about

it! He is your grandfather, he is your grandfather, he is your grandfather." In Afrikaans, "Jy het hom nie gekies nie. [You did not choose him.] He is there in your family." At the same time, he does not avoid the harsh truth, "There is that about him that he came to represent a vicious system, that he is seen as the symbol of a vicious system. . .though he wasn't alone in that. . . ."

I recall how some Black people were furious with Tutu during the TRC for his strong emphasis on the need to forgive. I am concerned that requests for forgiveness by people like me might have more to do with wanting to be freed from a burden of guilt than being rooted in a sincere commitment to restorative justice. Therefore, I am relieved when he hesitates, "This symbolism is part of the pain that you have to bear, I think until. . .I don't know when it will be that we will say, 'Yes, we have to forgive' and say 'he was a product of his time.'"

The Arch feels like the ideal person to ask about the symbolism of the Luthuli figure on the cross in the Black Christ painting:

Father, for me the spear represents the pain "my people" caused—we need to accept that pain, we cannot run away from that. The pain symbolized by the spear is the cross WE have to carry as the people my grandfather represented and as his family. But Chief Luthuli also had your generosity of spirit. Is there room, in my understanding of that icon, to accept that Luthuli also represents your—and so many other people's—generosity of spirit? That as a result of this generosity someone like me live with the pain we caused, but I am not rejected as a brother and a sister in Christ. And that gives me hope. . .

The Arch responded:

"Yes! I mean, you wouldn't survive, really, you wouldn't be able to live in this world if you didn't have to say that those two elements are there. Look at you, with your antecedents, that you could be what you are and be accepted into the TRC as part of the team. . . And, ja, it is just part of life, you will have to go to Mars to get away from pain that you have not caused directly. Just as much as you had nothing to do with the many good things you inherited."

He continues with this pastoral approach, with another thrice repeated dose of purified truth:

Do be careful that you don't want to take on a burden that is unbearable. Yes, acknowledge things that should be acknowledged. And then do what YOU can to make this world a world where such things will be more and more rare—the things that bring so much anguish to your heart. Seek to be what you are, to be someone who recognizes that human beings are human beings are human beings. That is already a massive renunciation of where your grandfather stood. When you are able to work with Black colleagues in the TRC and didn't have to use your Whiteness for benefits. You used your Whiteness mainly to help people get into the heart of some of the anguish. Don't smother your gifts with this burden. Let him being your grandfather make you sensitive to the position of people. And sensitive also to those White people who still want to play the race card, without being hoity-toity: Feel a sadness for them and hope that their eyes will be opened.

My precious time with this beloved spiritual parent is over. I stand up and greet him with both hands, "Thank you very, very much, Father. Thank you for your radical spirituality of including everyone. I hope you will be with us for many years to come!"

With a large smile and a warm handshake, "I don't know about that, the way things are with my health. . .One carries you in one's heart. *Ek gaan nie opstaan nie, boetie. Man, ek sukkel. . .ek is nou 'n ou man. . .*" [I'm not getting up, young brother. It is difficult for me . . . I am now an old man.]

"Do be careful that you don't want to take on a burden that is unbearable"

This tea with Father Tutu was indeed profoundly pastoral, without him avoiding the painful, prophetic truth conveyed by the centurion-with-a-spear in *Black Christ*: "There is that about him that he is seen as the symbol of a vicious system. . .this symbolism is part of the pain that you have to bear." I find it highly significant that he, as someone who is well known for his counter-cultural, unflinching conviction that "there is no future without forgiveness" (Tutu 1991), went on to stress that there is no closure in sight for someone like me to be relieved of this burden: "I think until. . .I don't know when it will be that we will say, 'Yes, we have to forgive' and say 'He was a product of his time.'"

He also emphasized, repeatedly, that his "generous judgment" of Verwoerd is not about exculpation or whitewashing. His hesitation to use the language of forgiveness draws an important distinction between Christ's "father forgive them" and the generosity of spirit of someone like Tutu, who, like Luthuli, represents those being crucified in *Black Christ*. I have become increasingly disillusioned by how White South Africans have domesticated Tutu's radical inclusivity and cheapened his forgiveness with "White ignorance" and avoidance of shared historical responsibility. Tutu's hesitance regarding forgiving Verwoerd, and those he represents, is for me an important reminder of the irreparability of transgenerational harm caused by the vicious system of apartheid and its colonial predecessors.

His "I don't know when" shines a sobering light on the never-enoughness of my restitutional responsibility.[8]

On other hand, I continue to be encouraged by his pastoral care—"Don't smother your gifts with this burden;" "Do be careful that you don't want to take on a burden that is unbearable." In what follows, I explore three angles on

---

8. For more detail on the complex dynamics of forgiveness and apology in contexts of deep political division, see Verwoerd and Little (2016, 2018). For more on the need for "everyday social restitution" by White South Africans see Swartz (2016); Verwoerd (2019).

how to make this White Verwoerd burden bearable, without looking, I hope, for premature relief. Firstly, I draw mostly on the above pastoral conversation to locate the burden of my embodiment within the ongoing mystery of the Incarnation. I then continue the conversation by, secondly, discussing how to share this burden through an expanded generational sense of self and time. Thirdly, I revisit my question to him about how to transform the pain represented by Black Christ *from a spiritual depth, not just at a political level.*

> "Let him being your grandfather make you sensitive to the position of people."

Father Tutu encouraged me to use my unavoidable grandfatherly connection to someone who has come "to represent a vicious system" as an opportunity for sensitivity training. He gave priority regarding the "position of people" on the receiving end of this vicious system— appreciating my "concern about the anguish and the pain that was caused by a policy" so closely associated with Verwoerd, namely "Grand Apartheid" or so-called "Separate Development." This policy intensified the systemic privileging of all South Africans classified as "White" at the increased expense of so-called "non-Whites." I therefore am glad that Father Tutu made the connection between me being a Verwoerd and the need for me to be careful how I use the undeniable "benefits" of "Whiteness." I am grateful that he saw my "work with Black colleagues in the TRC" as a way of using my "Whiteness mainly to help people get into the heart of some of the anguish."

Furthermore, he guided my sensitivity even in the direction of the position of Verwoerd as an Afrikaner political leader at that time—"We should not demonize them, whilst not exculpating them. They were under the pressures of their time: they had just come out of a bruising war; they had sought to escape from the British. . . ." And regarding Verwoerd, he admonished me to "be generous in your judgment of him. He was not a vicious man. . . ."

My sensitivity training is also to include the "position of people" in the present as well, even "those White people who still want to play the race card, without being hoity-toity: Feel a sadness for them and hope that their eyes will be opened."[9]

The radical inclusivity exhibited by Father Tutu in this conversation came from his deep commitment to follow in the steps of Jesus, the Christ, within the particular South African place and time he was born into. Through his example and pastoral care, he has helped me to accept my unique embodiment as more than an accident, as more than a heavy burden.

When Father Tutu encouraged me to use the "gifts" that come with my embodiment and the benefits that come with Whiteness (without being hoity-toity) to help reduce human anguish, he was also reframing the meaning of being a Verwoerd. He midwifed my growing understanding that being born into the Verwoerd family in the 1960s and racialized as a White person in apartheid South Africa is actually a reparative invitation: to transform our South African version of separatist superiority into

---

9. For more on this kind of faith-based "White work" see Van der Riet and Verwoerd (2022a, 2022b).

humanising "sensitivity" and compassion without boundaries; to follow Christ and, therefore, to participate in the mystery of the ongoing incarnation of God's love for the world.

Accepting this invitation to cultivate an incarnational sense of self has become critical in sustaining my capacity to bear the burden of my embodiment on the quest for deep (racial) transformation. On this quest, I am learning that participating in the incarnation includes the cultivation of a generational sense of self and time.

"He is your grandfather, he is your grandfather, he is your grandfather."

My current racial repair practice at Stellenbosch University (SU) is supporting the incarnational quest to "do what [I] can to make this world a world where [human anguish] will be more and more rare," without the weight of Whiteness personified by Oupa Hendrik becoming overwhelming. In the process I am internalising more deeply what it means, in practice, to accept Father Tutu's "he is your grandfather. . .he is there in your family," a family which includes my parents, children, and grandchild.

Following an ugly racist "incident" at Stellenbosch University (SU) in May 2022, my AVReQ colleague, Ayanda Nyoka, and I began to facilitate relational learning journeys for diverse groups of staff and students. These journeys are aimed at cultivating shared responsibility for deepening (intersectionally aware) racial transformation at the only remaining White majority higher education institution in SA, with a strong connection to the system of apartheid.[10] Our focus is the embodied, relational translation of SU's 2018 "Restitution Statement," which starts with this sentence: "We acknowledge [our] inextricable connection to generations past, present and future."[11]

Our personalized translation of this introductory sentence has been guided by Krondorfer's experiential application of Boulding's "200-year present" in settings of transgenerational intergroup conflict. For him the 200-year present is "a presence measured by physical touch," illustrated by him being touched by his grandparents, born around 1900, and him touching his future grandchildren, who may live into the decade of the 2090s. "From the 1900s to 2090s, this is the 200-year present of my life" (2020:49). In mixed groups of, for example Germans and Jews, he fruitfully introduced the 200-year-present by asking participants to create "embodied constellations" of the "generational chain of their family histories." In his experience, this constellation of the 200-year-present "can be very compelling because it conveys tangibly the effects troubled histories in families belonging to either victimized communities or a perpetrator society" (2020, 50).

His experience has been confirmed by us applying the 200-year-present in the context of SU. We ask participants to introduce pictures of the oldest person and the youngest person in their families that they have been/are "in touch" with. As a "participatory facilitator" (Little and Verwoerd 2013), I bring these pictures:

---

10. See https://www.sun.ac.za/english/CIRCoRe

11. For full Statement see https://www.sun.ac.za/english/about-us/strategic
-documents

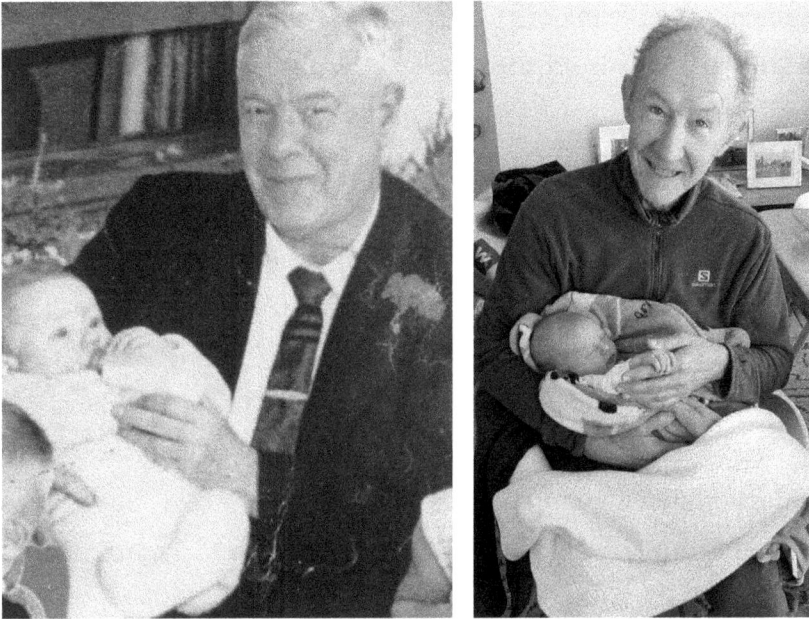

Figure 3: On the left, me as a 6 months old baby, being held by a grandfather; on the right, me holding my first grandchild.

Oupa Hendrik was born in 1901, Eli in 2022. If everything goes well, he could live till 2101. From 1901 to 2101—two hundred years connected by physical touch. This is my 200-year present. In similar fashion, we personalize the 200-year present for each participant before we begin to explore the very challenging application of this transgenerational sense of time and self to the implementation of the SU Restitution Statement.

From my point of view, this relational recognition of the "inextricable" connectedness between "generations past, present and future" leaves no room for individualistic denialism—my grandparents and parents and myself were included in a place such as SU because of the color of our skin; Myself, my children and grandchild(ren) continue to benefit from the exclusion of the majority of South Africans. The fact that *Oupa* Hendrik was also a professor at SU, as well as a prominent political leader, helps me to resist the temptation to privatize my 200-year-present, to rather locate my family history, with positional awareness, within the larger 200-year-present of a place such as SU. And when accepting retrospective generational responsibility for restitution becomes too heavy, I just have to shift my focus to the forward-looking dimension of my 200-year-present. Holding my grandchild's hand becomes a powerful encouragement to remember that my involvement in, for example, SU transformation, is also for his sake. So that SU becomes a place where he, and every grandchild of current staff and students, will be able to flourish.

However, I've found that even this generational broadening and lengthening of my sense of self is not strong enough to carry the burden Father Tutu was concerned about. The deepening of transformation requires a further deepening of my sense of self. I therefore need to return again to *Black Christ* and that pastoral tea conversation with Father Tutu.

> "Seek to be someone who recognizes that human beings are human beings are human beings."

Father Tutu's pastoral encouragement highlighted that the recognition of our shared humanity does not come easily—it requires a committed seeking, a "reparative quest" as my Tutu-like colleague, Pumla Gobodo-Madikizela, puts it. This quest applies to everyone who has internalized Whiteness—everyone who has been affected by the violence of colonialist "epidermalization" (Fanon 1970); anyone dehumanized by the "ultimate blasphemy" of oppression, sanctified by a White Jesus, that made many of those forcibly classified as "non-White" "doubt whether they were indeed God's children" (Tutu). And for those of us who followed this idolized Jesus and who share responsibility for this ultimate blasphemy, the reparative quest becomes a "massive renunciation' of where your grandfather [our ancestors] stood". Given the often intensely conflictual and confusing nature of this renunciation, I continue to be tempted to run away (Verwoerd 2019; 2022). Faced with the persistence of (inner and outer) apartheid in post-1994 South Africa, confronted with the ongoing relevance of *Black Christ*, I often am filled with despair.

In these moments of psychological "darkness," I am reminded by Father Tutu's example that *Black Christ* is ultimately grounded in the cross of Jesus, the Christ, as a paradoxical symbol of hope pointing to a "a dimension of life beyond the reach of the oppressor"(Cone). Including the oppressor in me. This message of hope can actually be found in the radiant gaze of the Luthuli figure in *Black Christ*, looking, with remarkable serenity, beyond the violence of apartheid represented by the centurions. My appreciation of this aspect of *Black Christ* is enhanced by locating it, thanks to De Gruchy and Louw (2014), within the long tradition of Orthodox icons:

Today, when human countenance is so disfigured, when racial discrimination persists, when so many people suffer from a lack of genuine, sincere communication, faces on the icons radiating a light that comes from beyond fascinate and beckon us to contemplate. Although they speak indeed of God, they also speak about humanity. (Quenot 2002:148, in De Gruchy 2008, 28)

From this perspective, Luthuli's gaze also radiates "a light that comes from beyond." And *Black Christ* "beckon us to contemplate" the inalienable iconicity of all human beings as image-bearers of God. In this way, *Black Christ* has become a "means of grace" on my oft-faltering quest to radically renounce what my grandfather, and I, stood for.

On this quest, I have also found that a beyond-icons, a beyond-words contemplative prayer life is vital to *sustain* my seeking to recognize, in practice, "that human beings are human beings are human beings." For this I am also grateful to Father Tutu. He introduced me, indirectly, to a stream of apophatic contemplative Christian spirituality (Williams 2019) that over the last thirty years have "rooted and grounded" me in "the love of Christ that surpasses knowledge" (Eph 3:14–19)—beyond the wordy, Scripture-focused, kataphatic, Reformed theology and piety that shaped my faith; beyond the reach of the constructed White, Afrikaner, Verwoerd dimensions of my being.

This introduction happened in the early 1990s at a time of spiritual crisis. I was so disillusioned with the DRC and the White "Christ" that shaped my faith into my early 20s, that I couldn't even find the language to pray to a Jesus that I could no longer imagine, to a God that felt very absent. I can't remember exactly how it happened, but during this "dark night of the soul" (May 2005), I ended up with the ecumenical Centre for Christian Spirituality, founded by Archbishop Tutu a few years before. Through this Centre, I found a spiritual director, Father Barry Grey, an Anglican priest, to guide me into a more spacious, beyond words experience of an infinite Caring Presence. And in the Centre's library, I discovered Thomas Keating, Richard Rohr, Anthony de Mello. Since that time, a daily "Centering Prayer" practice has become the taproot of my faith and my participation in the quest to deeply transform apartheid.[12]

I wish I had more time during that pastoral tea with Father Tutu to explore the contemplative dimension of his theology and spirituality. I found a promising hint in Tutu's back cover recommendation of Martin Laird's *Into the Silent Land: The Practice of Contemplation*:

> Often they say, "You learn how to swim by swimming," but a good coach or swimming manual is essential. Equally, we could say, "You learn how to be contemplative by contemplating" and a good guide or mentor is necessary. *Into the Silent Land* is just that. I tried it and it works. Try it.

It has also worked for me. I have revisited this book many times as a source of inspiration to poetically gesture towards a sense of self, "beyond the reach of the oppressor," that grows from persistent, mature contemplative practice:

> We discover in the process that there is more depth within us than we ever dreamt. There is not only chaos, confusion, emotional attachment, anxiety, and anger's nettled memory; not just the marvel of discursive reason,

---

12. See https://www.contemplativeoutreach.org/; Keating (2003).

imaginative insight, and unconscious instinct, but also an abyss of awareness that is always flowing with bright obscurity, grounding all these mental processes, one with all and one with God (Laird 2006, 70).

The "abyss" metaphor hints at a depth dimension within us as human beings that cannot be captured in words. However, abiding in this dimension, I have also found, requires a movement beyond metaphors of light and even "bright obscurity" into "sacred darkness," into the "thick darkness" of the cloud on mount Sinai where Moses met God (Exodus 19:3,9,16; 20:21; Feldman 2020; Verwoerd 2024, forthcoming). For, as Williams helpfully points out in *Seeking the God Beyond*, this apophatic darkness "paradoxically offers us a truer knowledge of God than light does—because in darkness we realize that we haven't grasped more than a fraction of the divine, whereas in light we are tempted to think we have seen all there is." Divine beyondness, for example in Gregory of Nyssa, "is not so much a matter of transcendence vs immanence as of infinity." For Gregory "divine infinity" means that "God is beyond time and space; God is not a being among others but the source of all being. God's goodness, creativity and love are endless because God has no end, no boundary, no limit." (2019, 77).

I also resonate strongly with Williams' emphasis on Gregory of Nyssa's "daring" application of the "infinity and unknowability of God to the human soul": "[W]e are made in relationship with God...and because our desire [for God] is infinite, we are in a sense never complete, never finished—there is always more of ourselves to be discovered in relationship with God.

We continue to be created, for ever… we can't exhaust God, or ourselves, in the journey or the dance" (2019, 80–81).

Since we are also made in relationship with each other, as affirmed in Tutu's universalist ubuntu (Battle 1997), this apophatic sense of being human has radical political and personal implications. On the one hand, the inexhaustible, infinite quality of human beyondness highlights the "ultimate blasphemy" (Tutu), the profoundly reductionist violence of apartheid, and any form of racism and colorism. On the other hand, the presence of divine beyondness around and within each "child of God," within and around each person "created in the image and likeness" of Infinite Love, provides the strongest possible source of hope to also sustain the quest for deep racial repair. For even though the localized Whiteness of apartheid is rooted in five hundred years marked by slavery and colonialism, the abyssal nature of this racialized suffering (Sharpe 2016; Santos 2018) is still limited in space and time. The psycho-social and moral "darkness" of apartheid as a crime and a sin against humanity cannot break the invisible, intimate, inclusive embrace of Infinite Compassion.

On a personal level, making the apophatic darkness of *The Cloud of Unknowing* (2009) my spiritual home (Verwoerd 2024 forthcoming) through decades of Centering Prayer has kept me grounded in this faith: there is a dimension to my being that runs deeper than the Afrikaner "Christian nationalist oppressors" blood on my hands, deeper than the White milk of separateness and superiority that shaped my bones, deeper than the "architect of apartheid's" genes in my body. And Father Tutu has helped me to remember that this radically inclusive depth dimension is also present in someone who became a prominent symbol of a vicious system: "Having said ALL of that, he was a human being like all of us."[13]

Saved by *Black Christ*, Tutu and the cross

Father Tutu's purified wisdom thus helped me "to face the pain represented in [Black Christ], without demonizing my grandfather." His prophetic pastoral care continues to guide my search "for ways how I can help to transform that pain, from a spiritual depth, not just at a political level."

In this chapter, I have highlighted how the transformation rather than the transmission of the "sins of the fathers" require the transformation of my sense of self. At the political level, this re-formation includes going beyond an individualistic, liberal sense of self towards an expanded self that accepts generational inextricability. And transforming "from a spiritual depth" includes internalising an incarnational sense of self. This depth dimension enables my embodiment to become bearable through a coming home to my body as, foundationally, another "temple of the Holy Spirit" (1 Cor 6:19). Doing *lectio divina* with this awe-inspiring metaphor takes me beyond its moralistic reduction to a puritanical warning against body-based "sins," towards an apophatic sense of self, with indwelling divine beyondness providing the unbreakable, all-embracing heart of human beyondness.

---

13. For an application of contemplative anti-racist activism in the USA context, from an African-American point of view, see Holmes (2016; 2021).

In conclusion, the deep transformation of the pain represented by my (generational, White) embodiment, also requires a complementary anchoring in the cross and *Black Christ*. I have found it very helpful to ground my contemplative practice in the mystery of the cross, aided by Cynthia Bourgeault. For her Centering Prayer is, theologically speaking, about following Jesus on his incarnational path of *kenosis* (Phil 2:9-16). This apophatic prayer practice is a daily "taking up of [my] cross": a dying to our egoic, kataphatic, sense of identity—a loving letting go of "our interior dialogue, our fears, wants, needs, preferences, daydreams and fantasies," gently and simply entrusting "ourselves to a deeper aliveness." This participation "in the death of Christ" is also a participation "in his resurrection," a "finding one's life"—during the period of Centering Prayer "we have not been holding ourselves in life, and yet life remains." She goes on to state that "[w]ith patience and persistence, these skills first patterned in [apophatic prayer] can be transferred to "real life." Through CP "it gradually becomes ingrained in us that 'losing one's life'. . .entails first and foremost a passage from our ordinary awareness to our spiritual one, because only at this deeper level of non-fearbased, wholistic perception will we be able to understand what is actually required of us. . .in the outer world." (81–83).

In understanding what is specifically required of me as a White Verwoerd, the *Black Christ*, mediated by Tutu and others, has helped me to follow Jesus in the "outer world" of post-1994 South Africa. Along this route of inner and outer, individual and collective transformation of inherited pain, *Black Christ* has indeed become a "means of grace," inviting me into a personalized, historically grounded, embodied experience of the paschal mystery.

My mediated acceptance that "the pain symbolized by the spear is the cross WE have to carry as the people my grandfather represented and as his family" still feels like a dying to my White, Afrikaner, Verwoerd self. But through a daily taking up *this* cross, I have also become more and more alive. This dying includes painful conflict with, especially, my father (Verwoerd 2019), but in the midst of being rejected as a family traitor, "someone like me [can] live with the pain we caused, [because] I am not rejected as a brother and a sister in Christ." Through the tangible generosity of spirit of those represented by Luthuli, I am given my daily bread—a deeply liberating taste of the "kindom" (Knitter 2009, 93) of heaven.

When I manage to let go of my anger, and the temptation to be hoity-toity, when faced with unrepentant children and grandchildren of the centurion-with-a-spear I do "feel a sadness for them and hope that their eyes will be opened." Remembering that this centurion is still in me, I wonder how White South Africans can join the circle of solidarity represented by the "Colored" Madonna and the "Asian" John standing with Luthuli on the cross of apartheid. Encountering *Black Christ* as an icon has also helped me to see that the route to genuine cross-racial solidarity requires a (re)conversion of White South African Christians (Jantzen 2020). This conversion includes, in my personal and professional experience, a laying down of our oppressive spears and a taking-off of reactive armour, that will allow us to get in touch with the beyondness, the infinite dignity, of (racialized) fellow human beings, including ourselves.

References

Anonymous, *The Cloud of Unknowing, with the Book of Privy Council*. Translated by Carmen Butcher. London: Shambhala, c.a., 2009.

Battle, M., *Desmond Tutu: A Spiritual Biography of South Africa's Confessor*. Louisville,

Kentucky: Westminster John Knox Press.

Battle, M., *Reconciliation: The Ubuntu Theology of Desmond Tutu*. Cleveland: Pilgrim, 1997.

Biko, S., *I write what I like*. Johannesburg: Picador, 2012.

Boesak, A., *Black and Reformed: Apartheid, Liberation and the Calvinist Tradition*. Johannesburg: Skotaville, 1984.

Boulding, Elise, "Expanding our Sense of Time and History: The 200-Year Present" in J.R. Boulding (ed.), *Elise Boulding: A Pioneer in Peace Research, Peacemaking, Feminism, Future Studies and the Family*. New York: Springer, 2017 (1988), 155–158.

Bourgeault, Cynthia, *Centering Prayer and Inner Awakening*. Chicago: Cowley Publications, 2004.

Cone, J.H., *The Cross and the Lynching Tree*. New York: Orbis Books, 2017.

Davenport, T.R.H., *South Africa: A Modern History*, Johannesburg :Macmillan, 1986.

De Gruchy, J.W., *Liberating Reformed Theology: A South African Contribution to an Ecumenical Debate*. Grand Rapids, Michigan: W.B. Eerdmans, 1991.

De Gruchy, J.W., *Christianity, Art and Transformation: Theological Aesthetics and the Struggle for Justice*, Cambridge: Cambridge University Press, 2001.

De Gruchy, J.W., *Being Human: Confessions of a Christian Humanist*. London : SCM Press, 2006.

De Gruchy, J.W., *Icons as a Means of Grace* Wellington: Lux Verbi, 2008.

Fanon, F. *Black Skin White Masks*. Paladin, 1970.

Feldman, F. "To Dwell in the Thick Darkness: The Sacred Dark in Jewish Thought" in *Anima Mundi. Voices from Many Shores (An Anthology of Spiritualities)*, Frederique Apffel-Marglin and Stefano Varese (eds.). New York: Peter Lang, 2020, 181–206.

Gobodo-Madikizela, P., "What Does It Mean to be Human in the Aftermath of Mass Trauma and Violence? Towards the Horizon of an Ethics of Care" in *Journal of the Society of Christian Ethics 36*(2), 64–91.

Gobodo-Madikizela, P. "The afterlife of apartheid: a triadic temporality of trauma" in *Social Dynamics*, 49(1):67–86.

Hansen, L. *The legacy of Beyers Naudé*. Stellenbosch: SUN Press, 2005.

Harrison, R., *The Black Christ: A Journey of Freedom*. Cape Town: David Philip, 2006.

Holmes, Barbara. *Joy Unspeakable: Contemplative Practices of the Black Church*. Minneapolis, MN: Fortress Press, 2017.

Holmes, Barbara. *Crisis Contemplation: Healing the Wounded Village*. Albuquerque, NM: CAC Publishing, 2021.

Jantzen, M. R. "Neither Ally, Nor Accomplice: James Cone and the Theological Ethics of White Conversion." *Journal of the Society of Christian Ethics* 40, no. 2 (2020): 273–290.

Keating, T. *Intimacy with God: An Introduction to Centering Prayer*. New York: Crossroad Publishing, 2003.

Kenney, H. *Architect of Apartheid: H.F. Verwoerd—an Appraisal*. Johannesburg: Jonathan Ball, 1980.

Kleinschmidt, H., ed. *White Liberation: A Collection of Essays*. Johannesburg: Spro-Cas, 1972.

Knitter, P.F. *Without Buddha I Could Not Be a Christian*. Oxford: Oneworld Publications, 2009.

Kritzinger, K. "Liberating Whiteness. Engaging the Anti-Racist Dialectic of Steve Biko." In *The Legacy of Stephen Bantu Biko: Theological Challenges*, edited by C.W. du Toit, 89–113. Pretoria: Unisa, RITR, 2008.

Krondorfer, B. *Unsettling Empathy: Working with Groups in Conflict*. London: Rowman & Littlefield, 2020.

Laird, M. *Into the Silent Land: The Practice of Contemplation*. London: Darton, Longman and Todd, 2006.

Lentz, R., and E. Gateley. *Christ in the Margins*. Maryknoll, NY: Orbis Books, 2003.

Little, A., and W.J. Verwoerd. *Journey through Conflict Trail Guide: Introduction*. Victoria, BC: Trafford Publishing, 2013.

Louw, D.L. *Icons: Imaging the Unseen*. Stellenbosch: SUN Press, 2014.

Luthuli, A. *Let My People Go: The Autobiography of Albert Luthuli*. Cape Town: Tafelberg, 2006.

May, G.M. *The Dark Night of the Soul: A Psychiatrist Explores the Connection between Darkness and Spiritual Growth*. San Francisco: HarperSan Francisco, 2005.

Mofokeng, T.A. *The Crucified Among the Crossbearers: Towards a Black Christology*. Kampen: J.H. Kok, 1983.

Report of The Truth and Reconciliation Commission of South Africa, vols. 1, 4. Cape Town: Juta Press.

Swartz, S. *Another Country: Everyday Social Restitution*. Cape Town: Bestred, HSRC Press, 2016.

Thesnaar, C. H., and L. Hansen, eds. *Unfinished Business? Faith Communities and Reconciliation in a Post-TRC Context*. Stellenbosch: African Sun Media, 2020.

Tutu, Desmond. *No Future Without Forgiveness*. London: Rider, 1999.

Quenot, Michael. *The Icon: Window on the Kingdom*. Crestwood, NY: St. Vladimir's Seminary Press, 2000.

Santos, B. de S. *The End of the Cognitive Empire: The Coming of Age of Epistemologies of the South*. Durham, NC: Duke University Press, 2018.

Sharpe, C. E. *In the Wake: On Blackness and Being*. Durham, NC: Duke University Press, 2016.

Van Wyngaard, G.J. "White Christians Crossing Borders: Between Perpetuation and Transformation." In *Unsettling Whiteness*, edited by L. Michael and S. Schulz, 191–202. Oxford: Inter-Disciplinary Press, 2014.

———, "In Search of Repair: Critical White Responses to Whiteness as a Theological Problem – A South African Contribution." Doctoral dissertation, Vrije University Amsterdam, 2019.

Verwoerd, W. J. *My Winds of Change*. Johannesburg: Ravan Press, 1997.

———, "On Our Moral Responsibility for Past Violations." *Alternation* 8, no. 1 (2001): 219–242.

———, "Towards Hospitality between Enemies." In *Debating Otherness with Richard Kearney: Perspectives from South Africa*, edited by D.P. Veldsman and Y. Steenkamp, 287–306. Cape Town: AOSIS, 2018.

———, *Verwoerd: My Journey through Family Betrayals*. Cape Town: Tafelberg, 2019.

———, "Transforming (Christian) Apartheid." In *Reconciliation, Forgiveness and Violence in Africa: Biblical, Pastoral and Ethical Perspectives*, edited by M.J. Nel, D. A. Forster, and C. A. Thesnaar. Stellenbosch: SUNMedia, 2020.

———, "The Black Christ and White South African Responsibility After 1994." In *Historical Trauma and Memory: Living with the Haunting Power of the Past - Conference Proceedings*, edited by

P. Gobodo-Madikizela, E. Ndushabandi, and K. Ratele, 77–92. Stellenbosch: SUNMedia, 2021.

———, "Blessed Are the Peacemakers? Enemy Love, Family Hatred and the Dynamics of Betrayal." *Spiritus: A Journal of Christian Spirituality* 22, no. 2 (2022): 212–231.

———, "'Be Sure You Make Your Home in This Darkness': The Cloud of Unknowing and the Unlearning of 'White Unknowing.'" In *Embodying Theology: Spirituality and Justice*, edited by Lisel Joubert and Ashwin Thyssen. Stellenbosch Theological Reflection Series. Wellington: Bybelmedia (forthcoming), 2024.

Verwoerd, W.J., and A. Little. "Public and Private: Practitioner Reflections on Forgiveness and Reconciliation." In *Reasonable Responses: The Thought of Trudy Govier*, edited by C. Hundleby, 148–173. Windsor, Ontario: University of Windsor, 2016.

———, "Beyond a Dilemma of Apology: Transforming (Veteran) Resistance to Reconciliation in Northern Ireland and South Africa." In *Reconciliation in Global Context: Why It Is Needed and How It Works*, edited by B. Krondorfer. New York: SUNY Press, 2018.

Van der Riet, L.R., and W. Verwoerd. "Diagnosing and Dismantling South African Whiteness: 'White Work' in the Dutch Reformed Church." *HTS Theological Studies* 78, no. 4 (2022a): 1–9.

———, "Intergenerational 'White Work' in the Dutch Reformed Church: Settling Conflict, Unsettling Continuity." In *Faith, Race and Inequality Among Young Adults in South Africa: Contested and Contesting Discourses for a Better Future*, edited by Nadine Bowers-Du Toit, 25–40. Stellenbosch: SUN Media, 2022b.

Williams, R.L. *Bonhoeffer's Black Jesus: Harlem Renaissance Theology and Ethic of Resistance*. Waco, TX: Baylor University Press, 2014.

Williams, J.P. *Seeking the God Beyond: A Beginner's Guide to Christian Apophatic Spirituality*. Eugene, OR: Wipf and Stock Publishers, 2019.

Wolterstorff, N. "The Wounds of God: Calvin's Theology of Social Justice." *The Reformed Journal* 37, no. 6 (1987): 14–22.

CHAPTER SEVEN

We Are Made for Harmony, for Interdependence

Thabo Makgoba, Archbishop of Cape Town and the Province of Southern Africa

Three decades ago, my predecessor-but-one as the Anglican Archbishop of Cape Town, Desmond Mpilo Tutu, spoke perceptively about the changes the world was undergoing in the wake of the changes introduced by the reforms of Mikhail Gorbachev.

Addressing the Carnegie Corporation of New York in January 1992, he outlined a vision of a moral foundation for human society in the future based on biblical insights. He emphasized in particular how "the Bible places human beings at the center of the divine enterprise as creatures of infinite worth and dignity with a high destiny, because each is created in God's image to be not just respected but indeed held in awed reverence as a God-carrier destined for life with God."

With this in mind, he was enthusiastic about the potential offered by the developments which began late in 1989 in venues such as St. Nicholas Church in Leipzig, which hosted some of the protesters who eventually brought down the German Democratic Republic in the eastern part of the modern Germany.

"What tempestuous days, what momentous days we are living through," he told the Carnegie audience:

> We are rushing through quite epoch-making changes at breakneck speed and we can be forgiven for being somewhat breathless and possibly sometimes bewildered. We have been seeing history in the making in an extraordinary fashion. . .
>
> In a matter of a few years, the geopolitical and physical map of the world has changed before our very eyes. Quite incredible, that there is now no longer a USSR. In its place is a commonwealth of independent republics striving after democracy and a free market economy. . . There is no Iron Curtain any longer for there is no Eastern bloc. The Warsaw Pact has been dissolved and the Cold War has ended.
>
> What a remarkable turnaround. There is now no longer a West Germany because the initiative of Mr. Gorbachev led to the fall of the Berlin Wall and now Germany has been reunited. Familiar landmarks, physical and spiritual, have disappeared and we are to a large extent perplexed. There must be a paradigm shift because we have all been accustomed to the categories and thought and behaviour patterns of the Cold War. We are needing to undergo a Copernican revolution in all our thinking and conduct.[1]

---

1. Desmond Tutu, Address to the Carnegie Corporation of New York, January 1992. (Unpublished manuscript.)

Accentuating the positive effects of the realignment of international forces, Tutu added: "Quite remarkable things have become possible, which we were dreaming about, which we and others were praying for and many others fought and suffered and were imprisoned for and went to exile and even died for."

He was of course referring partly to what was happening in South Africa; now unable to appeal to Western anti-communist sentiment, and suffering the effects of sanctions and low levels of investment, the incoming South African president, F.W. de Klerk, was forced to release Nelson Mandela and his fellow leaders, allow exiles to return, lift the bans on our liberation movements and begin negotiations for democracy.

Less apparent to Tutu's Western listeners were the reforms sweeping across Africa at the time. Referring to what has since been labelled as Africa's "second wave" of liberation, in which the number of multi-party democracies were to grow from five in 1989 to 36 in 1995, he cited developments in Angola, Namibia, Mozambique, Benin, Zambia, Eritrea, Ethiopia, Algeria, Kenya, Togo, Zaire (now the Democratic Republic of Congo), Nigeria, and Ghana.

Giving a Western perspective on the events of that time, Francis Fukuyama famously proclaimed "the end of history," adopting Hegel's thinking that history is headed for an endpoint, and arguing that a liberal democracy with a market economy is the ideal form of political organization to which to aspire.[2] Many Westerners hoped, as Gillian Hart has written,

---

2. As described by the Australian academic Chris Fleming: https://theconversation.com/the-end-of-history-francis-fukuyamas-controversial-idea-explained-193225.

that "[t]he end of the Cold War was supposed to usher in the global triumph of neoliberal capitalism combined with secular liberal democracy."

Instead, we saw the rise of religious fundamentalism and competitive nationalisms, most dramatically seen in the geo-political arena in the war which led to genocide in the Balkans. Desmond Tutu addressed the problem in his Charge to the Provincial Synod of the Anglican Church in Southern Africa in 1995. In a section headed, "Transition, Violence, Fundamentalism, and Xenophobia," he wrote:

> Periods of transition almost by definition are times of instability because well-known landmarks have been shifted or removed and people feel they have thus lost their bearings. They then are allergic to diversity and difference and consequently seek homogeneity (and hence so-called ethnic cleansing). What is different, or the stranger, these are not tolerated easily and we tend to look for often simplistic answers to what are usually fairly complex issues. All kinds of fundamentalisms become the vogue. We look for refuge in churches and organizations where adherents toe a particular line because no-one is usually permitted to dissent. There is a nostalgia for an absolute certainty that is really illusory.[3]

From my vantage point at the southern tip of Africa in 2024, it appears to me that the world is again going through

---

3. Desmond Tutu, *Charge to the Provincial Synod of the Anglican Church of Southern Africa*. September 1995. (Unpublished manuscript.)

a time of epoch-making changes, one in which revolutionary technological advances which have the power to achieve great good also threaten to tear humanity apart. As Hart added, although "[s]ince the early 1990s, increasingly financialized capitalism has continued to metastasize around the globe. . . we have also witnessed the explosive growth of racist and xenophobic expressions of nationalism and authoritarian right-wing populist politics in many different regions of the world, often linked to the rise of religious fundamentalisms and invocations of 'family values.'"[4] We have also seen the growth of an unbridled capitalism in which reckless lending in pursuit of profit generated a global financial crisis. Perhaps most damaging to people in Western democracies, banks threatened with collapse were deemed too big to fail, so governments used the people's money to bail them out while thousands of home-owners were ruined.

In international relations, the conflicts which fundamentalism and xenophobia have generated appear to have borne out Samuel P. Huntingdon's predictions of a "clash of civilizations" as the post-Cold War world order is re-made. In Huntingdon's assessment, "[a]lignments defined by ideology and superpower relations are giving way to alignments defined by culture and civilization. . ., [c]ultural communities are replacing Cold War blocs, and the fault lines between civilizations are becoming the central lines of conflict in global politics."[5]

---

4. Gillian Hart, "Resurgent Nationalisms & Populist Politics in the Neoliberal Age," *Geografiska Annaler: Series B, Human Geography* 102, no. 3 (2020): 233–38. doi:10.1080/04353684.2020.1780792.

5. Samuel P. Huntingdon, *The Clash of Civilizations and the Remaking of World Order* (Simon & Schuster, 1996), 125.

As followers of the Prince of Peace, who came so that all "may have life and have it in abundance" (Jn 10:10), this is profoundly depressing. But in his 1995 Synod address, Tutu offered another way of looking at our plight. Responding to the gloomy prognostications arising from the divisive and polarizing effects of the end of a bi-polar world order, he argued that the world we inhabit is "a great deal more perplexing and complex" than a resort to fundamentalisms allow for. Far from the changes being a problem, he said, instead they "make. . . it so exhilarating to work out things for oneself rather than operate by rule of thumb". Returning to the Bible, he added:

> Our Lord appeared to opt for a different approach. He refused to give the lawyer a list of those who were his neighbours, but instead told the story of the Good Samaritan as if to say life is too exhilarating, too fascinating, too perplexing for it to be lived by rote. We are constantly having to make choices and the evidence is not always so clear-cut and overwhelming that it makes stringent thinking superfluous.
>
> I hope we will remember that Jesus said the scriptures bore witness to Him and therefore He is the Word of God par excellence. We should ask, 'What is the mind of Christ? What would Jesus say or do in this particular set of circumstances?'

Adopting this approach, what do we as Anglicans, as Christians, as people of faith, have to offer our world as we navigate the 21st century? More specifically, what do those of us from the Global South have to offer the Anglican Communion and the ecumenical and inter-faith communities as we all struggle together to discern the mission and the ministry to which God calls us in the 2020s and 2030s?

Two preliminary points are needed. First, it is important to record that, thankfully, in an era of climate change which threatens to overwhelm us all, we have in the past 30 years developed a better understanding of how abundant life for all means not just abundant life for humanity but for all of God's creation; that our theology now recognizes that our environment is not something to be exploited or ignored, but that it forms, with us, part of what Desmond Tutu called "the bundle of life." We need to keep that constantly in mind.

Secondly, I proceed from the assumption that, at least in the Anglican Communion, we recognize that the era in which doing theology is dominated by Western theologians is over.

Some years ago, when I was writing a memoir which included an account of my ministry to Nelson Mandela during his last years, I had cause to reflect on how the Communion's history is tied to the spread of European colonialism, to the way in which colonists and settlers overwhelmed—and in many places, wiped out—the lives of indigenous peoples, and to the suffering inflicted by long-lasting practices, from slavery, to denial of the franchise, to systems such as apartheid. This has been no more dramatically highlighted recently (2024) than by the discovery in the Lambeth Palace Library archives that in the 18th century, Archbishop Thomas Secker of Canterbury approved reimbursements for the purchase of enslaved people to work on sugar plantations in Barbados owned by the then Society for the Propagation of the Gospel in Foreign Parts (SPG).[6] (Archbishop Justin Welby has written movingly of how a visit to Cape Coast, Ghana, from where the enslaved were dispatched to the Americas, had reminded him of how "the abomination of transatlantic chattel slavery was and has always been blasphemy."[7])

Desmond Tutu has pointed out how missionaries often destroyed traditional culture when they first came to evangelize in Africa. Preaching at the 150th anniversary of the mission founded in the Northern Cape of South Africa by David Livingstone's father-in-law, Robert Moffat, he remarked:

> [O]ften we have criticized missionaries because they were seen often as one arm of the imperial might of European expansionism. We are often unhappy that they thought being European was synonymous with being Christian; that they often made our people ashamed of being African, [believing] that God would not usually hear your prayers if you were African unless you were dressed in European clothes; that often they destroyed our rich cultural traditions.[8]

6. https://www.churchtimes.co.uk/articles/2024/31-may/news/uk/newly -found-ties-between-lambeth-and-slave-trade-painful-but-important-says -archbishop-welby

7. https://www.archbishopofcanterbury.org/news/news-and-statements ·/archbishop-canterbury-slavery-healing-and-justice-all

8. Desmond Tutu, *Excerpt from a sermon preached at the Kuruman Moffat Mission,* October 9, 1988. (Unpublished manuscript.)

My own social-political and cultural context is rooted in the northern-most province of South Africa. I come from the Tlou clan of the Sepedi-speaking people, who dominate much of the north of modern-day South Africa. The earliest surviving written records of my clan's existence show that in about 1800 we moved to a beautiful valley which came to be called Makgoba's Kloof (an approximate translation of *kloof* would be "gulf"). There, my great-grandfather, Kgoši (King) Mamphoku Makgoba, ruled our clan in peace until, first, the British defeated a powerful neighbour of ours, the famed Sekhukhune of baPedi (the Pedi people), and then Dutch-speaking settlers of the Zuid-Afrikaansche Republiek defeated the British. Soon afterwards, settlers of European heritage began to invade our land, either in search of gold or to peg out farms for themselves. My great-grandfather resisted, ordering our people to destroy the settlers' beacons and to refuse to pay the taxes they tried to levy. He was taken hostage and first jailed in a portable "iron fort." However, he simply dug his way out, buying the clan a few more years of freedom. Finally, in 1895, the settler republic sent its troops after him. They recruited commandos across from six districts of the republic, raising more than 4,000 men to search the forests of the ravine for our clan's few hundred soldiers. After a number of inconclusive clashes, Swazi auxiliaries caught up with us on a Sunday, when the settlers' commandos were at church in a nearby town. Once the auxiliaries had found Kgoši Makgoba, they decapitated him and took his severed head to town to prove they had killed him. Our clan was the last-but-one to be crushed by colonial or settlers' regimes in South Africa. (We are still trying to trace our king's skull, most recently in Germany, where we suspect it might have been taken as a memento.)

During the writing of my memoir, I was asked why—given the treatment of indigenous peoples across the world by people who called themselves Christian—was I a Christian? This was my reply:

> I am a Christian and I remain a Christian because I remember that our faith begins with a young Palestinian on a donkey. I draw this phrase, and some of my reflections on it, from the memoir written by Denise Ackermann entitled "Surprised by the Man on the Borrowed Donkey."[9] The image conjured up by Denise's title tells me that since Roman times we have perverted the Word and the mission of Jesus Christ, and its message about what God is up to in our world. Over the centuries we've allowed ourselves to be pointed to imperial agendas. Christ's message has been attached to national flags, to military might and to the AK-47.
>
> But that is not the gospel. Christianity is not imperialism. Christianity is not colonialism. Christianity is how do I love my neighbour as myself and as others. The man who links us to God is he who enters Jerusalem a nonentity, riding a borrowed donkey. He is humble and he is marginalized but his message of love and simplicity is powerful; it is powerful enough to challenge the

---

9. Denise Ackermann, *Surprised by the Man on the Borrowed Donkey* (Lux Verbi, 2014).

perversion of common humanity that empire engenders. It tells the Roman Empire that God's kingdom is not about creating an economic system that crushes an agrarian people. The Christian identity I aspire to is one of equality, harmony, reconciliation, truth and, indeed, one of turning the other cheek. For me that is more persuasive and forceful than the values of those who hold secular power.[10]

I draw support for my approach from the history of the church in other parts of Africa, where it was not a by-product of colonialism. The Coptic Church's calendar begins in AD 284, the Nubian church's history officially dates back to AD 543, and the Ethiopian monastic movement was founded towards the end of the fifth century.[11] Identifying ourselves within this context enables me to declare myself "a proudly African Christian," able to join on equal terms, Anglicans and other Christians elsewhere in Africa and the world who are called to find better ways of promoting the Kingdom of God in church and society both within and between nations.

Moreover, there are admirable cases of Anglicans of European descent who not only displayed minds open to learning from the indigenous people among whom they ministered but went on to defend their leaders against colonial oppression. One such was John Colenso, the first Bishop of Natal, whose dialogue with his

---

10. Thabo Makgoba, *Faith and Courage: Praying with Mandela* (SPCK, 2019), 188.

11. Bengt Sundkler, Christopher Steed, *A History of the Church in Africa* (Cambridge University Press, 2000), 11, 30, 36.

assistant and confidant, William Ngidi, in the mid-19th century led him to develop new thinking aimed at bringing about what he called "a complete Revolution in the religious tone of England." His writings—which expressed more tolerance for polygamy than was customary at the time, and questioned the literal accuracy of the Bible based on his study of the Pentateuch—led my earliest predecessor as Bishop of Cape Town, Robert Gray, to find Colenso guilty of heresy and excommunicate him.[12] Colenso and his daughter, Harriette, went on to defend the Zulu monarchy in the face of the depredations of British colonialism.[13] After the British overthrew King Cetshwayo kaMpande and occupied Zululand in 1879, Colenso observed that they had made the name of Englishmen "in the Native mind the synonym for duplicity, treachery, and violence."[14] When the British were ruling Palestine under a League of Nations mandate in the 1930s, British missionaries were prominent among those who protested when British forces—including the notorious "Black and Tans" who had fought against republicans in Ireland—wantonly killed civilians, blew up villages and tortured suspects.[15] In southern Africa, the stellar examples of Anglicans who stood with us in our struggle for liberation were, of course,

12. Jeff Guy, *The View Across the River: Harriette Colenso and the Zulu Struggle against Imperialism* (University Press of Virginia, 2002), 21–28.

13. Ibid. *The View Across the River* is a detailed study of Harriette Colenso's defence of the monarchs, particularly of Cetshwayo and his son, Dinuzulu kaCetshwayo.

14. Jeff Guy, *The Heretic: A study of the life of John William Colenso, 1814–1883* (Ravan Press and University of Natal Press, 1983), 287.

15. Caroline Elkins, *Legacy of Violence: A History of the British Empire* (Alfred A. Knopf, 2022), 194–197, 232, 237.

Trevor Huddleston of the Yorkshire-based Community of the Resurrection, who supported us in South Africa, and Michael Scott, who campaigned for Namibian freedom at the United Nations.[16]

Missionaries also pioneered education and health facilities for indigenous communities, which Tutu acknowledged in his sermon at the Kuruman Moffat Mission:

> But I do want to pay a very warm tribute to some truly remarkable and fearless people who dedicated their lives to their Lord and Master, who were willing to leave their relative comfort at home, to face the unknown, the mysterious and the dangers of foreign lands. Many, many, many of us would not be alive today had it not been for the hospitals and the clinics and the health education and care that the missionaries pioneered.
>
> Many, many, many of us owe the fact of us having been educated at all to the indomitable men and women who blazed the trail to provide education for the Africans when the secular authorities were less than enthusiastic and who would hardly have been able to cope with the growing needs of the black population.
>
> And more than anything, we give thanks to God for them for bringing us the Gospel of salvation through faith, faith in the life and death and resurrection of Our Lord and Saviour Jesus Christ. It is an unsurpassable

16. Robin Denniston, *Trevor Huddleston: A Life* (St. Martin's Press, 1999); Entry on Michael Scott in *The Dictionary of African Christian Biography*, https://dacb.org/stories/southafrica/scott-michael/

gift. We have come to learn that we too, all of us, are of inestimable worth. We have a worth that is intrinsic to who we are, a worth that does not depend on extraneous attributes such as race and wealth and status and skin color.[17]

I believe that our history as churches of the Global South, with our experience of both oppression at the hands of colonial power and our resistance to oppression which led to the steady decolonization of the way in which we express our faith, enable us to make an important contribution to bring about the "equality, harmony, reconciliation, truth and. . . [capacity to turn] the other cheek" of which I have written. There is a wonderful Sepedi phrase which is evocative of our potential for the world, and that is: *Sekgo sa Metse*. Literally translated, it simply describes water in a jug—*sekgo* is a vessel and *metse* is water. Yet the phrase has a much deeper meaning, just as the phrase "living water" in John's Gospel describes the Holy Spirit. *Sekgo sa Metse* not only provides drink for the thirsty, it also transforms different ingredients into sustaining nourishment, and having done so, it provides *thlabego*, yeast, which catalyses the next meal to come. In short, Christians in the Global South are well placed to help our world bring about the human flourishing which is implicit in Christ's promise of abundant life.

At times, this means that we will have to express our differences clearly to our sisters and brothers of the Global North. I did this at the 2024 General Convention of The

---

17. Tutu (1988), Moffat Mission sermon.

Episcopal Church in the United States, when speaking at a dinner for the outgoing Presiding Bishop, Michael Curry. I felt open to share with them my journey of struggle and the differences between our churches, so I noted on the one hand that we in the Province of Southern Africa are still struggling after 30 years to agree on ways to provide pastoral ministry to people living in the same-sex civil unions recognized under South Africa's 1996 Constitution. But I also felt free to add a little yeast (*tlhabego*), challenging them to engage more actively in the Palestinian struggle for justice and democracy. At the end of a Convention which had declined to take a position on whether Israel is an apartheid state, I made clear that those of us who actually lived under apartheid—and also had extensive experience visiting Israel and Palestine—have no doubt that Israel, especially in the Occupied West Bank, practices apartheid as defined under international law.

Against Huntingdon's thesis of a clash of civilizations, the South African journalist and author, Allister Sparks, has posited an approach to ending conflict based on the African world view of *ubuntu*, or *botho* in my mother tongue. *Botho* says that "a person is a person through other persons," or "I am because you are; you are because we are."[18] Desmond Tutu has expressed beautifully the potential this philosophy holds for the world:

Westerners are very good at pulling things apart, at breaking them down with their analytical skills. Look

18. Translated from the phrase, in my mother's home language, "Motho ke motho ka motho yo mongwe."

at their scientific achievements. But they aren't so good at putting them together. Africa has a gift to the world that the world doesn't have, really, the gift of saying that the strict individualism of the West is debilitating. We can't boast about it because it's a gift from God, but the world is going to have to learn the fundamental lesson that we are made for harmony, for interdependence.[19]

(Well before the church as a whole adopted its current focus on the integrity of creation, Tutu extended his analysis to cover the natural world as well:

The world is discovering we are made for interdependence not just with human beings; we are finding out that we depend on what used to be called inanimate nature. When Africans said, "Oh, don't treat that tree like that, it feels pain," others used to say, "Ah, they're pre-scientific, they're primitive." It is wonderful now how they are beginning to discover that it is true—that that tree does hurt and if you hurt the tree, in an extraordinary way you hurt yourself.[20]

Sparks says that the Western powers have failed to understand adequately the causes of the "fundamentalist religious and ethnic backlash" which has caused so much conflict in the beginning of the current century. Through "failed military strategies" they have only "sown further destabilization and confusion" by

---

19. Desmond Tutu, *The Essential Desmond Tutu* (Mayibuye Books, 1997), 70.
20. Ibid.

making "ill-considered attempts to impose democratic order on. . . unappreciative societies. . ."[21] Instead, he has written, the world needs to pursue "a deeper understanding of the complexity and validity of other major religions and cultures—of 'otherness' generally."

Leaders in the Global South can play an important role in pointing to new ways of promoting common understanding and defusing conflict. As Sparks suggested, the world's wealthiest nations, in material if not in spiritual terms, have little understanding of how the ways in which they wield their power alienate nations and peoples which—while they may have cultural and spiritual strength—are economically and militarily much weaker. Our experience of oppression at the hands of the powerful enables us, for example, to educate them on centrality of justice as the basis on which the world can appropriate the true peace which Jesus leaves us (Jn 14:27). As I write, we see this playing out in front of our eyes in the resilience of Palestinians in the face of oppression and in South Africa's case in the International Court of Justice accusing Israel of breaching the Convention on the Prevention and Punishment of the Crime of Genocide, adopted by the United Nations in 1948.[22]

In the same vein as Tutu, Steve Biko, the leading exponent of black consciousness, wrote in 1973: "We believe that in the long run the special contribution to the world by Africa will be in

21. Allister Sparks and Mpho Tutu, *Tutu Authorized* (HarperOne, 2022), 289–290.

22. https://www.ohchr.org/en/instruments-mechanisms/instruments/convention-prevention-and-punishment-crime-genocide

this field of human relationships. The great powers of the world may have done wonders in giving the world an industrial and military look, but the great gift still has to come from Africa—giving the world a more human face."[23]

Desmond Tutu has observed that when he studied in London in the 1960s, the predominant theological voices at the time assumed that the theology they practised was theology. When he suggested to Geoffrey Parrinder of King's College, renowned for his studies of comparative religions, that he would like to write a doctoral thesis on black theology, Parrinder asked what black theology was. "He asked the question in a tone of voice that made it clear he had no doubt at all that it was obvious there could be no such entity," Tutu wrote later.[24] So when in 1972 the Taiwanese theologian, Shoki Coe, introduced the concept of "contextualizing" theology as a means of liberating it from Western thought, he "roiled the pond of missiological thinking," as Ray Wheeler has written.[25] Coe's pioneering work on the methodology of contextualization has become the "mother of contextual Theologies," reinforcing the legitimacy of the theologies developed by the Global South in the last 50 years.

When I was installed as Archbishop of Cape Town in 2008, I spoke of the need to "seek afresh to discover what it is to be the body of Christ in our time, and who God is in Jesus Christ,

---

23. Steve Biko, *I Write What I Like* (Picador Africa, 2018), 51.

24. John Allen, *Rabble-Rouser for Peace: The Authorized Biography of Desmond Tutu* (Free Press, 2006), 135.

25. Ray Wheeler, *The Legacy of Shoki Coe* (International Bulletin of Missionary Research, 26(2), 2002), 77–80. https://doi.org/10.1177/239693930202600205

for us here and now."[26] To seek afresh what it is to be the body of Christ in the 21st century necessarily means doing theology in our current context—a context in which, at the global level, the powerful nations of the world are failing to give answers as to how to achieve the true peace which is represented by the word *shalom* or *salaam,* the peace which the prophets Jeremiah and Ezekiel had in mind when they denounced political and religious leaders for speaking of "Peace, peace" when "there is no peace" (Jer 6:14, 8:11 Ezek 13:10). Stated briefly, we need to mobilize the resources of our faith, and the theologians of the Global South need to step up if the people of God are to help the world find the answers the world needs.

Moreover, for Anglicans to step up in pursuit of these aspirations is to act in accordance with our finest and oldest traditions: what Michael Ramsey has described as the central place which the Incarnation holds in Anglican theology. Since I was installed as archbishop, I have come to realize its centrality for me, too, and I have returned to it again and again as a lens through which to explore theology and its relation to the world around us. For me, its importance is rooted in John's Gospel: "In the beginning was the Word, and the Word was with God, and the Word was God... And the Word became flesh and lived among us..." (Jn 1: 1,14) Austen Kaiser notes that Archbishop Ramsey traced the role of the Incarnation in our theology back to Richard Hooker: "Ramsey located the origins of the Anglican Incarnational tradition (which he described as

---

26. https://archbishop.anglicanchurchsa.org/2008/03/archbishop-thabo -makgoba-installion-at.html

'first place in Anglican theology. . . through the centuries') in Hooker's strictures against the condemnation of society and the natural world as evil or ungodly in themselves."[27] Speaking to the Keswick Convention in 2007, John Stott suggested that some in his audience might "immediately recoil in horror" from his contention that "we are to be like Christ in his Incarnation." He continued:

> Surely, you will say to me, the Incarnation was an altogether unique event and cannot possibly be imitated in any way? My answer to that question is yes and no. Yes, it was unique, in the sense that the Son of God took our humanity to Himself in Jesus of Nazareth, once and for all and forever, never to be repeated. That is true. But there is another sense in which the Incarnation was not unique: the amazing grace of God in the Incarnation of Christ is to be followed by all of us. The Incarnation, in that sense, was not unique but universal. We are all called to follow the example of His great humility in coming down from heaven to earth. So Paul could write in Philippians 2:5–8: "Have this mind among yourselves, which was in Christ, who, though he was in the form of God, did not count equality with God something to be grasped for his own selfish enjoyment, but emptied

---

27. Austin Elliott Kaiser, *Michael Ramsey, Archbishop of Canterbury: Incarnational Anglicanism and British Society, 1928–1974* (Dissertation for Doctor of Philosophy degree, Department of History, University of Oregon, 2012), 73. https://scholarsbank.uoregon.edu/xmlui/bitstream/handle/1794/12367/Kaiser_oregon_0171A_10355.pdf

himself, taking the form of a servant, being born in the likeness of men. And being found in human form he humbled himself and became obedient unto death, even death on a cross." We are to be like Christ in his Incarnation in the amazing self-humbling which lies behind the Incarnation.[28]

In Toronto in 2011, I described Jesus Christ, as God incarnate, as "our ultimate model of what it is to be fully human." I added:

Human flourishing is to grow in Christ-likeness not merely in some overly spiritualized way but also in the flesh and blood realities of the fullness of life. This must be the goal to which all of mission—and indeed, all of politics in its broadest sense—is directed. This is the so-called "common good" of which we may speak. It is a matter of eternal values not so much being made concrete as being incarnated, finding human expression among those who are made in God's image, enjoying the wonders of God's creation, as God purposed for us.

In other words, the Incarnation communicates to us that God is, so to speak, on our side. In Christ Jesus, God demonstrates God's solidarity with the human condition. He is with us, alongside us, and, more than that, one of us—to a degree we probably will never adequately

---

28. John R.W. Stott, *The Model: Becoming More Like Christ—John Stott's Final Address* (Knowing & Doing, C. S. Lewis Institute, Fall 2009), https://www.cslewisinstitute.org/wp-content/uploads/KD-2009-Fall-The-Model-Becoming-More-Like-Christ-610-1.pdf

understand this side of heaven. So, no matter what we face, God is with us. God is in the midst of this or that situation, among these and those people, desiring we all find abundant life in him. There is nowhere where he is not present, nowhere where he cannot work for good. Nor are we, as Christians, ever alone, in our vocation to be the body of Christ, in all situations and among all people: Jesus is with us as we seek to meet others in their needs; and in reaching out to them, we should also expect to encounter him already present there.[29]

Bringing this home to my context in southern Africa, I told our Province's 2016 Provincial Synod:

Simply put, by incarnation I refer to God in Jesus entering the everyday experience of human living to point us to God's reign and to prepare and invite us through our everyday lives to enjoy the blessedness of this reign. My writing and advocacy on the theme of the Incarnation and politics is born out of the struggle of God's people with political systems in southern Africa that demeaned all of us and which were not designed to address the concrete needs and experiences of our daily lives or to respond to God's call to human flourishing.[30]

---

29. Snell Lecture, Cathedral Church of St James, Toronto, 30th October 2011; https://archbishop.anglicanchurchsa.org/2011/11/snell-sermon-incarnate -jesus-christ-in.html

30. https://archbishop.anglicanchurchsa.org/2016/09/archbishops-charge -to-provincial-synod.html

Looking at how the Communion could contribute to bringing about the justice on which true peace is built, we can of course extend my southern African reference to the world—where we can make a contribution to the struggles of God's people everywhere against the political, economic and military systems which powerful nations use to keep the rest of us in subjugation.

Our economic systems illustrate the crisis the world faces. In South Africa, I frequently refer to the way in which, despite the defeat of apartheid and the introduction of democracy in 1994, we have still not achieved an economic liberation to match political liberation. Our economy is distinguished by intergenerational inequality, in which those who are likely to flourish in our society are the sons and daughters of the elite, who enjoy a good education and have the contacts to help them advance in their careers, and the daughters and sons of the poor, who struggle to break out of a vicious circle of poverty and disempowerment.[31] The African National Congress, the party of Nelson Mandela, lost its majority in the 2024 national elections after ruling for 30 years precisely because it has failed to provide equality of opportunity. We are, according to the Gini index calculated by the World Bank, the most unequal society in the world, in which a few top earners enjoy a high proportion of the country's income, in contrast to the small proportion earned by the vast majority.[32]

------

31. Ibid.

32. https://data.worldbank.org/indicator/SI.POV.GINI?locations=ZA &most_recent_value_desc=true

But, as the index shows, the problem is not confined to South Africa, or the other nations best known for income inequality, such as Brazil or the United States. It affects us all to one degree or another. That is why I found so encouraging the first-ever Ecumenical School on Governance, Economics and Management inaugurated by the World Council of Churches, the World Communion of Reformed Churches, the Council for World Mission and the Lutheran World Federation in Hong Kong in 2016. The basis for our discussions there was outlined by the organizers: "An economic system based on over-consumption and greed has become firmly rooted in today's world and it is high time to change this paradigm by working for a new financial and economic architecture."[33] At the meetings, we looked at how the worldwide Christian community could help stimulate a new "economy of life" to replace the current form of global governance of money and financial systems. Instead, we said, we want a system which will transform the market economy from a self-serving mechanism for elites to one which serves our environment and all the world's people.

If we as Africans are to fulfill the role that Biko envisaged for us, we must put into practice the philosophy of *botho* or *ubuntu*. In my 2019 memoir, I wrote that accepting that "a person is a person because of other persons" means that I cannot be fully human unless I recognize your humanity fully, and that as Africans we try to organize ourselves "on the basis of relationship rather than structure or legislation." I observed:

---

33. https://www.oikoumene.org/news/current-and-future-church-leaders -gather-for-gem-school-on-new-financial-and-economic-architecture

Jesus said: 'Do not think that I have come to abolish the law or the prophets; I have come not to abolish but to fulfil' (Matthew 5.17). And how does Jesus tell me, Thabo, to fulfil the law? Not primarily by following rules. Rather by loving God with all my heart and all my soul and all my mind, and by loving my neighbour as myself. 'On these two commandments hang all the law and the prophets' (Matthew 22. 37–40).[34]

As Nelson Mandela and other leaders of his generation showed us in South Africa in the early 1990s, Africans can offer, indeed have offered, the world a model of how to reconcile and live in peace together. Desmond Tutu did it by working in meetings, even on the most controversial issues, on the basis of consensus, an African style of leadership which he explained during a visit to West Africa in 1990:

> It is not true that our chiefs were dictatorial, because almost everywhere in Africa the good chief was the person who could listen and then draw a consensus. Consensus happens because people have their different points of view and the good ruler says, "I have listened to all of you, we are not taking a vote, but listening to you I think most of you are feeling that we must go this way rather than that way." Now the ruler who could discern what the people wanted was the ruler who lasted on his throne.[35]

---

34. Makgoba, *Faith and Courage*, 196.
35. Tutu, *The Essential Desmond Tutu*, 67.

Thus, in an acknowledgement of the need to embody African symbolism and theological concepts in the way we operate as a Communion, at the 2008 Lambeth Conference we adopted the African methodology of *indaba,* in which we talk through issues at length until we reach a consensus view on the most difficult of them.

However, right now we as African Anglicans are not fulfilling our potential to bring people together, not least because we are not living by our own values. Instead, and this happens especially over our differences in the debate over respect for different expressions of human sexuality, we are placing ourselves in different little boxes, isolated from one another, driving us apart and detracting from our credibility as bridge-builders. As I argued in my memoir, "If we are to bring African values to the Communion, surely we should maintain ties of fellowship, using those attributes which come naturally to us: forming relationships, wrestling with one another, not running away from one another?"[36] For instance, why can't we look at the debate over human sexuality through the lens of contextual theology and see it as a pastoral matter? If we accept that one of our principal responsibilities as those who aspire to act as the Body of Christ is to provide ministry to our people, can we not accept that their pastoral needs differ according to the culture in which they live, and that the nature of the ministry they require will therefore differ in different cultural settings?

To fulfil our potential as Anglicans and Christians to be a light to the nations, we need to come together to address the

---

36. Makgoba, *Faith and Courage,* 194, 197, 199.

common challenges we face on a global, regional and local level: poverty and inequality; rapid technological changes; protection of the environment and natural resources; interfaith and intercultural cooperation; strengthening democracy and social justice; and addressing the causes of migration and refugees. We must work to foster better understanding of the complexity of these challenges, to strengthen mutual cooperation and trust and to facilitate common action through partnerships.

I was recently asked by the Anglican Communion Office in London for a reflection on what inspires me about being part of the global family that is the Communion. My reply sums up my aspirations for us as the Body of Christ:

> What I love about the Anglican Communion is the way in which, in our relationships with one another and by respecting the dignity of difference, at our best we beautifully reflect the glorious diversity of the children of God across the world. In spite of our often vast differences in human experience and in the environments in which we live, our deep theological heritage, steeped in Scripture and interpreted through reason and tradition, binds us together. Taking the Incarnation seriously, we don't shy away from the everyday lives of our sisters and brothers, instead rolling up our sleeves and getting our hands dirty for those on the margins, even as we also share the Good News with the wealthy and the privileged. Like any family, we have differences—which we sometimes voice loudly and passionately. But through Communion partnerships and exchange programmes, we

learn how much we need one another, and we overcome our differences when we respect how our varied societal contexts call for differing pastoral approaches as we give expression to God's glory through our mission and ministry.

.

www.ingramcontent.com/pod-product-compliance
Ingram Content Group UK Ltd.
Pitfield, Milton Keynes, MK11 3LW, UK
UKHW021929260825
2763IPUK00006B/12